ICEBERG SLIM

A Biography of America's Most Notorious Pimp

By: Richard Lewis

© **Copyright 2019 - All rights reserved.**

The content contained within this book may not be reproduced, duplicated or transmitted without direct written permission from the author or the publisher.

Under no circumstances will any blame or legal responsibility be held against the publisher, or author, for any damages, reparation, or monetary loss due to the information contained within this book. Either directly or indirectly.

Legal Notice:

This book is copyright protected. This book is only for personal use. You cannot amend, distribute, sell, use, quote or paraphrase any part, or the content within this book, without the consent of the author or publisher.

Disclaimer Notice:

Please note the information contained within this document is for educational and entertainment purposes only. All effort has been executed to present accurate, up to date, and reliable, complete information. No warranties of any kind are declared or implied. Readers acknowledge that the author is not engaging in the rendering of legal, financial, medical or professional advice. The content within this book has been derived from various sources. Please consult a licensed professional before attempting any techniques outlined in this book.

By reading this document, the reader agrees that under no circumstances is the author responsible for any losses, direct or indirect, which are incurred as a result of the use of the information contained within this document, including, but not limited to, — errors, omissions, or inaccuracies.

Table of Contents

Introduction 1

Chapter 1: Early Life 5
   A Young Boy's Eyes View A New Party 7
   An Education Is A Roadblock 10

Chapter 2: Dipping His Feet in A New Life 13
   A Taste of Prison 15
   Trying for a Different Road 20

Chapter 3: The Birth Of A Young Man Known As Cavanaugh Slim 25
   Off to Chicago 29
   Slim's Most Influential Hero 31
   Slim Finally Realizes His Dream 38

Chapter 4: A Halt In Slim's Pimp Dream 41
   Leavenworth Federal Penitentiary 44

Chapter 5: Back On The Fast Track 49

It's Gonna Be A Jailbreak 53
Back Into The Game 56
    Off To Detroit 57
    Slim's Stable Moves 58
    History Catches Up To Slim 62
    Slim's Decision 64

Chapter 6: To Turn In A Different Direction 66

To Find A Wife 67
Another New Beginning 72
Beck Becomes A Father 75

Chapter 7: Writing, Music, and Films 78

In Need Of A Publisher 80
From Pimp To Best Selling Author 83
From Novels To Film 93

Chapter 8: End Of An Era 96

Times Are Looking Up 99
Beck: Everyone's Father Figure 105
Beck's Growing Concerns For The African American Community 107

Chapter 9: The Legacy Iceberg Slim Left Behind. 114

Conclusion 121

Introduction

The life of a pimp is one that is portrayed often on the Hollywood screen today. However, this was not always the case. In fact, about fifty years ago, this type of lifestyle was rarely discussed. It was a form of taboo. Many people believed, that the only type of person that would do such a thing as becoming a pimp was someone who wasn't worth anyone's time. In the eyes of many, this type of person wasn't intelligent, had no talent, was addicted to drugs, received very little education, had no family, and was going nowhere in life. Then, one day in 1967, this all started to change because of one man. To the world, he would become known as Iceberg Slim. He was born Robert Maupin but would die Robert Beck.

The book that would start to bring the ghetto African American and pimp world into focus was called Pimp: The Story of My Life. It was written by a man who had been a pimp. It wasn't written to glamourize that type of lifestyle. It wasn't written to tell people to go out on the streets and become a pimp. It wasn't written as a beginner's guide to that lifestyle. It was written because Beck didn't want others to follow in his footsteps. It was written because he wanted to find a way to put that part of his life on the top shelf and not have to look at it again. It was written so he could try to forgive himself for what he did to his mother and the hundreds to possibly thousands of women he pimped out over the course of nearly 25 years.

While some people, including some African American organizations such as the Black Panthers, would become heavy critics of Beck's work, many other people would idolize it. However, they rarely enjoyed the book because they wanted to become the greatest pimp of their lifetime, they enjoyed the book because it gave them a sense of hope in their own lives. To many people, especially young African Americans, this book gave them hope that they could make something of their life. For some, it gave them hope that they could get off the streets and get an education or a better career. It gave them hope that they could raise a family. Most importantly, it made them feel like there was someone there who cared about them; someone there who wanted to see them succeed and be happy. For many young people in the late 1960s and into the early 1970s, this was an important piece that they were missing in their lives.

While you're reading this book, you might start to wonder how someone who became so cruel could have an inspirational life. The answers to this are right in this book.

This is a biography of a man who is best known as Iceberg Slim. A man who achieved his career goal of becoming one of the top pimps on the streets of Chicago during the 1950s. A man who lived in different prisons for over five years. A man who started to cope with his emotional pain through the use of drugs like cocaine. It's a story of someone who was ruthless. Someone physically, mentally, and emotionally abusive to hundreds of women throughout his lifetime. It's the story of a man who many people don't want to read about. However, it's also a story of a man who turned his life around and found a way to help other people get off the streets. It's the story of a person who used his mistakes to help better the lives of other people. It's one of the rare stories in the world that isn't often told, until now.

Today, you're more likely to find the names Iceberg Slim, Robert Maupin, or Robert Beck in articles and books. Even five years ago you wouldn't find his name as often as you do now. In fact, one of the most popular biographies about Robert Beck came out in 2012. For years, the name Iceberg Slim was only heard being spoken about by a few celebrities, by listening to gangsta rap, or reading books from the Urban Fiction or Street Literature genre. But, over the last few years, this has all started to change due to a few people who continued to hold on to Robert Beck's legacy in the hope that, at some point, the rest of the world would start to pay attention to who this man really was.

This book will give you a glimpse of who Iceberg Slim or Robert Beck really was. This book will follow Beck from the time he was born, through his childhood struggles, onto the streets of Milwaukee and Chicago, into the prison system, and then his journey towards becoming a different person. Through this book, you will read about Robert Maupin, Cavanagh Slim, Iceberg Slim, and Robert Beck. While he went by different names throughout his life, he was technically one person. This book will describe him by the name he was going by at the time. Therefore, in his early life, you will read about Robert Maupin. Once he starts his journey into the underground world you will read about Cavanagh Slim. Then, once he leaves the underground world behind, you will read about Robert Beck, who took the pen name Iceberg Slim as he didn't want to use his real street name in his books. Beck's names are written in this way because, as you will see, with each name he became a different person. It's a way to honor the man and his legacy that he left behind.

Chapter 1

Early Life

There are many stories of triumph and success throughout the course of history and everyone's story is different. Some stories are seen as more "rags to riches" stories while other stories focus on criminals who turned their life around after their prison release. The life of Robert Beck, better known as Iceberg Slim, is one of these stories. Not many people would expect that the story of a man who pimped out hundreds of women over two decades could become a triumphant story. However, Robert Beck's story fits this mold.

Iceberg Slim was born Robert Lee Maupin (sometimes written as Moppins) on August 4, 1918, in Chicago, Illinois. After's Maupin's father, Robert Maupins Sr. left, Mary Brown, Maupin's mother, moved herself and her son to Rockford, Illinois with a man known as Henry Upshaw. Before Henry came into their lives, Mary struggled to feed herself and her son. While Henry wouldn't become the answer to their wealthy prayers, a young Maupin started to adore Henry. In fact, Maupin stated in his autobiography, *Pimp: The Story of My Life* that he adored Henry as much as Henry adored his mother. Henry owned his own business in Rockford, which was something every African American man dreamed of during the Great Depression.

Living with Henry, Maupin learned that life didn't have to be full of financial struggles. He started to learn that not everyone needed to wonder where their next meal was coming from. In his autobiography, Maupin wrote highly of Henry who treated Mary like his queen. Anything that Mary wanted, Henry did whatever he could to make sure it would happen. On top of this, Henry treated Maupin like his own child. Maupin remembered how kind, caring, and religious Henry was. He discussed how the family would go to church every Sunday where Henry would thank God for his blessings in life.

It didn't take long for Maupin and Mary to get used to the middle-class lifestyle Henry gave them. They would walk into public places dressed as neatly as the doctors and lawyers. Mary started to get involved in community clubs and talk about her dream of owning a beauty shop. And, as Henry always did, he made sure it happened. And it didn't take Mary long to find a different male interest.

It was around this time that Mary started dating a street hustler known as Steve, who she left Henry for. While Steve didn't seem violent at first, it didn't take long for him to start showing his violent tendencies. Once this happened, Maupin not only started having troubles with Steve but also his mother. The young Maupin couldn't understand why his mother would stay with a man that abused both him and his mother. Unfortunately, the violence continued to increase until Mary ended up in the hospital with a broken jaw. Maupin believed that the only good that came out of that incident was that Steve ran off and mother and son never heard from him again.

A Young Boy's Eyes View A New Party

Mary recovered, the family moved into an attic apartment and she continued her dream at the beauty shop. At this point, Maupin started noticing a world he had never seen before, the world of pimping. Looking out the attic window, he would see various women out on the streets. He would see various men controlling these women. It didn't take long for Maupin to realize that there was a "horror house" across the street from his attic apartment. He became mesmerized by the flashy clothing the men would wear.

One of the biggest influences towards the lifestyle Maupin would one day find himself in was a pimp he called "Party Time" in his first autobiography, *Pimp: The Story of My Life*. Party Time wasn't the type of person parents would want their child to look up to. By the time Maupin met him, Party Time had spent time in jail. On top of that, Maupin knew Party

Time was a pimp. He had seen a piece of this lifestyle in action as a young boy looking out the attic window.

When a young Maupin saw Party Time, a woman, and another man together, he went outside to get a closer look at the people who he referred to as "freaks" in his autobiography. However, once he got a closer look at them, he noticed there was nothing different about them at all. He noticed they were clean and dressed nice. In this moment, Maupin realized that the people he believed were freaks when watching from his attic window, were just like anyone else on the street when he sat down outside.

At the time, Maupin grabbed an opportunity to talk with Party Time, mainly out of curiosity. As he sat there and listened to Party Time talk about what a great pimp he was, Maupin couldn't help but start to like the guy. After all, Maupin was new to the area and in need of someone to talk to and Party Time had interesting stories.

This was not the last time that Maupin would see Party Time. In fact, the two would start to meet when Maupin got out of school. Party Time would explain what Maupin would do and then, on a night when Mary was out working, Maupin and Party Time would put the plan into action.

This is the point when Maupin's real crime started. Party Time would help him dress up like a woman. He would then have Maupin stand in a dark alley as he looked for someone interested in the woman Maupin was pretending to be. Once Party Time found his victim, he would receive the cash and tell the victim to head towards Maupin. Not long after, each of these victims would be beaten and robbed.

Maupin not only saw pimps and their women in the places across the street from his home regularly but he also saw them in his mother's beauty shop. Her main clientele came from the people who lived in the world Maupin started to dream about. The women would come in and get their hair done for their night's work. He watched the men and noticed how they wore some of the nicest and most expensive clothing, hats, and jewelry he had ever seen. He noticed how the women looked with their makeup done well, revealing yet nice clothing, and fancy jewelry. At this point, Maupin had lived in poverty and had a middle-class lifestyle and he knew what type of lifestyle he wanted for himself. He didn't want to worry about where his next meal came from or how he was going to pay rent. He wanted to live a life of luxury; the same life that he saw his mother's clients live.

An Education Is A Roadblock

Education was an important piece of Maupin's young life. His mother knew that in order for him to get out of the ghetto, he would need an education. On top of that, Maupin was known to be intelligent. School seemed to come pretty easy for Maupin throughout his elementary and then high school years. In fact, Maupin graduated high school early, at the age of 15, and as one of the top students.

However, no one was sure what Maupin was going to do after graduation. His mother hadn't put much thought into making sure her son got a college education because they didn't have the money to pay for it. But, to his mother's surprise, an opportunity for Maupin to go to college was knocking on their door.

A lot of people knew that Maupin was someone special, including a group of graduates from Tuskegee University, a predominately African American college founded by Booker T. Washington. The alumni of Tuskegee told Mary that she wouldn't have to worry about her son's college expenses as they would take care of everything. She was so thrilled at the chance to see her son get a good education that he was sent to the university as soon as he could enroll.

Unfortunately, for Maupin, education was not on his mind. He didn't take it seriously and was more attracted to the girls than the books. He fell for several girls and had his mind on the lifestyle he saw across the street from his attic window. The lifestyle that his once friend, Party Time, had shown him.

Maupin dressed nice and slick. He was learning how to play the part of the lifestyle he had seen as a child but had no idea how to get started in it. Plus, it was nearly impossible for him to try as a 15-year-old boy. Even so, Maupin continued his ways with the girls at Tuskegee, even after it got him into trouble.

In the middle of his Sophomore year, he met a 15-year-old girl who adored him. At the same time, he was seeing another teenage girl. One day, he offered to meet the 15-year-old, but then never showed up. The next day, she had heard about his ways with other girls and found him in the main section of the campus. Maupin was caught and soon found himself in front of the school principal, who told him that the board was considering his dismissal and his mother had been informed of his actions. The principal called him a disgrace to the school and said he couldn't leave the campus at all.

But, the threat of dismissal disappeared as the alumni, who paid for Maupin to go to the school, found out about everything. This allowed Maupin to continue on the path he was taking. It also allowed him to find different ways to make money. Maupin, who was still a minor, couldn't follow the lifestyle of a pimp. Yet, he still missed having the money that he saw when he hung out with Party Time. He dreamed of being able to find a way to make that type of money again - or more. He wanted to go back to his mom's home and make people jealous of all the money he produced at Tuskegee.

Maupin thought he'd found a way when he struck a deal with someone over moonshine. Maupin was in charge of getting the supplies and selling it. He found someone who would help them with the supplies and getting started. Then, when it came time to sell it, Maupin asked some of the girls he had sexual relations with to sell the alcohol in their dorm halls. Eventually, too many people heard what was going on and Maupin was, once again, caught. This time, no one could save Maupin and he was sent home in the middle of his Sophomore year. It was also during this time that Maupin would get another taste of the pimping lifestyle.

Chapter 2

Dipping His Feet in A New Life

Not long after Maupin returned home after being expelled from Tuskegee University, his mother changed jobs. Because Mary had to live where she worked, she only made it home once a week. Maupin quickly learned that his mother would only be home on Sunday afternoons, so he found other places to stay during the week. The first placed happened to be with an ex-pimp and murderer known as Diamond Tooth Jimmy.

Maupin quickly found Jimmy to be one of his biggest influences. Jimmy was honest about the life he used to lead and often told Maupin fascinating stories about being a pimp. Because Jimmy ran a gambling house, Maupin quickly learned how to gamble as well as getting another taste of the pimp lifestyle. Other than what Party Time taught Maupin, he had always been amazed by the pimps who would bring beautiful women into his mother's salon. He wanted their lifestyle. He wanted to wear the fancy clothes they wore and be able to spend money however and wherever he wanted to.

Through observing the men and women, he came to learn that the world of pimping would bring in the money he desired. He didn't catch on to the control that he saw pimps have over their women, at least not right away. In fact, as he turned 17 years old, he continued to romance a girl two years younger and clean Jimmy's gambling joint as a way to earn his keep and make a living. However, this would all change one night when Maupin was lying next to his 15-year-old girlfriend.

He asked her to do him a favor. She responded that she would do anything for him. In return, Maupin got up and went to find someone he knew would go for the girl. He told this man that she was worth $5. He gave Maupin $5 and she did what she was supposed to do for the money. It was at this moment that Maupin realized that he could, even at 17 years old, find a way to make the money he desired. While he had always been in awe of the lifestyle, he wasn't fully sure that was the direction he was going to take. All he knew is that he wanted to make money, he wanted to make it fast, and he wanted to make a lot of it.

Maupin continued to find people who would be willing to do something with the girl. This would become Maupin's first big mistake as a pimp. One night he found a male who was willing but when he saw the girl, the guy immediately realized that he knew her. In return, he called the girl's father and Maupin got arrested.

Mary couldn't believe that her child would do such a thing. She supported her son and told everyone that it was a setup and he was completely innocent. However, no matter what Mary said, her son remained in jail and she had to find a lawyer. She found a lawyer through an old friend. Unfortunately, he wouldn't be able to help Maupin in any way as the girl's father was wealthy and had connections in the court system. Before the trial, he met with the judge and pulled some strings to make sure that Maupin would be locked away.

At the trial, the judge sentenced Maupin to no more than 18 months but more than one year at a local reformatory. Mary was distraught by her son's sentencing as the judge told Maupin he hoped this sentence would change his ways. He wanted Maupin to come out a changed man and stay off the streets.

A Taste of Prison

Even though the judge called the place a reformatory, Maupin makes it clear in his autobiography that it was a prison. His cellmate was someone he knew from school, who he called Oscar. While Oscar and Maupin hadn't gotten to know each other while at school, they would spend their time in the reformatory together.

Maupin's time in the reformatory was something he wouldn't wish on anyone; however, it wouldn't be enough to keep him from going back to prison in the future. From the beginning, he never cared for the food. In fact, at first, he could barely hold down a meal. On top of this, he dealt with bed bugs and the gut-wrenching smell of a cell without a working toilet.

But the smell, food, and bed bugs were only a few of the things Maupin had to deal with. He also had to deal with the officer who carried a cane. It didn't matter what the officer said, every single inmate needed to follow his instruction or he would hit them over the head with the cane. Maupin did everything he could to follow the rules. In reality, he was still a scared young child who missed his mother and his freedom. At the time, he didn't see himself as a criminal, he saw himself as a teenager trying to make his way in the world. He believed that he had gotten the raw end of the deal because he was an African American who grew up in the ghetto and the 15-year-old girl came from a wealthy family with pull in the criminal justice system.

Maupin also knew that he wasn't the only one who got the raw end of the deal. His cellmate had received the same sentence, one year in the reformatory because he had had sexual relations with a young white girl. According to Oscar, the two were dating, but when the girl's father found out, he pressured her into saying that Oscar raped her. The judge told Oscar the same thing he told Maupin, that he was too violent for society and hoped that at least a year in the reformatory would straighten him out.

Maupin felt sorry for Oscar. In fact, he worried more about Oscar than he did himself. He knew that Oscar wasn't like him. He really wasn't some criminal like Maupin was. Oscar had truly gotten the raw end of the deal. Oscar had grown up in a church and came from a decent family. Maupin often watched and heard Oscar praying, especially when he was frightened, which seemed to be more often than when he wasn't.

After spending six months in the reformatory, Maupin met someone who knew of Party Time, who had wired him a note. Upon reading the note, Maupin learned that Party Time had never forgotten about him and offered to help him in any way he could upon his release from the reformatory. Maupin was more than happy to receive such a letter from Party Time. He had always enjoyed their time together and looked up to Party Time like he had his mother's former husband, Henry.

As Maupin started dreaming about the type of life he would have when he got out of jail, Oscar continued to pray and read his Bible. Over time, Maupin started to notice that the officer who often checked on them was starting to become annoyed by how often Oscar read his Bible. Therefore, Maupin asked Oscar to stop so he wouldn't cause any trouble between him and the officer. Maupin truly started to worry about what the officer would do to Oscar. However, Oscar told Maupin not to worry about him because he was always protected by God. While this didn't ease Maupin's fears for Oscar, he also realized that there was nothing he could do.

Maupin's fears for Oscar came true one day as they worked to clean up. They were sweeping and mopping when Maupin was given two hotdogs from an inmate friend of his. Maupin gave one to Oscar, who put it in his pocket, and then snuck into a closed location to eat his. While the two men were finishing up, the officer with the cane came in and saw Oscar slowly eating his hotdog. Immediately, the officer started beating Oscar with the cane. Maupin tried to step in, wanting to help his friend but received a couple of hits himself. He then focused his attention on Oscar, who was laying on the floor moaning and all bloody. As people rushed in to help, Maupin noticed the officer smiling at the damage he had done to Oscar. This was the first time he had seen the officer smile and he started to realize that the officer's dislike for Oscar had nothing to do with his Bible or prayers. The officer knew about Oscar's girlfriend and wanted to seek his own revenge. After all, Oscar's girlfriend was not only two years younger but also crippled. She had been completely innocent until, according to the officer, Oscar had taken that innocence away.

Sometime later, Maupin would once again get Oscar as a

cellmate. He was beyond excited and couldn't wait to get back to his cell on the day Oscar was set to arrive. However, Maupin was disappointed once he saw what the beating had done to Oscar. Upon entering his cell, he saw someone he only recognized because of the scar on the side of his head. Oscar had received such a beating that he was no longer mentally able to function as he used to. He didn't remember Maupin and did nothing but sit in the corner of the cell by his bathroom bucket and spread the contents of the bucket onto the wall of the cell.

At first, Maupin tried to help Oscar. He wished that Oscar would remember him along with the fun and comfort the pair had given each other while they were locked up. Unfortunately, this wasn't to be and Maupin quickly realized he couldn't help Oscar. In fact, he couldn't live in the same cell with Oscar anymore. Therefore, he notified the officials and explained Oscar's actions inside the cell. While it bothered Maupin to see Oscar taken away to a nearby psychiatric hospital, he knew that he could no longer help him.

Maupin looked forward to his mother's weekly letters and monthly visits, especially now that Oscar was gone. If there was any reason he regretted the actions that had brought him to spend time in the reformatory, it was knowing the pain he caused his mother. Mother and son had a good relationship and even though Maupin didn't believe in God as strongly as his mother did, he still respected her. Maupin also wanted everyone to know how much his mother loved and cared for him. Therefore, he told her that she needed to call the warden at least once a week to let him know that someone out there cared about him. This was one of the only ways he could prove to the officials in the reformatory that he wasn't worthless.

A couple of months after Oscar was taken away, Maupin went in front of the parole board and received the okay to get released. He couldn't believe the news but became increasingly excited. However, one of the members of the parole board didn't seem so pleased as he told Maupin that they all knew they would see him again. In Maupin's mind, at the time, he knew they were wrong. He never dreamed of being in jail again. He was released a couple of weeks later and went back to his mother's home in Milwaukee, Wisconsin.

Trying for a Different Road

After his release, Maupin met with his parole officer and went to live with his mother. She had gotten him a job as a delivery person for her business neighbor, who owned a drug store. While Maupin wasn't too excited about the job, he took it. He wanted to stay out of jail, which meant he needed a job as this was one of the terms of his probation. He wanted to try to stay away from the lifestyle of pimping. However, he also found himself often thinking about that world, especially when he continued to see all the beautiful women who came into his mother's salon.

Eventually, his desires would catch up with him. One day, Maupin was sent on a delivery miles away from the drug store. Once he reached his destination, he fell head over heels for the lady who answered the door. While she didn't care too much for Maupin, she was interested in finding someone to do anything she wanted because her significant other was going to be gone for at least another week. Therefore, Maupin worked his way into her house and she found Maupin to be satisfactory to her desires.

Maupin would receive more than he ever thought as he stepped through the woman's doors. He quickly found out that she had been a prostitute and knew the profession well. She took Maupin in as one of her students and taught him everything she knew. He would continue to go and see the lady as often as he could. He started to learn what buttons to push to get what he wanted.

During one of their times together, she would teach Maupin something that he would carry with him for the next couple of decades. After Maupin slapped the woman across the face, she turned around and bit him. While he immediately curled up in pain, she came back to him and started showing him how he could turn the pain into pleasure. From that moment on, Maupin was hooked on this idea. He couldn't believe how something that he considered painful could bring him pleasure. Another door had opened in Maupin's mind.

Slowly, the cleaner road that Maupin was trying to follow disappeared. After his time with the lady, he wanted more of the pimp lifestyle. However, his views had changed a little bit. He didn't just want the lifestyle for the money. He also wanted it for the things that she had taught him. He wanted it for the pleasure that could be found in pain. On top of that, he also wanted it for the control that he could have over women. Maupin was now 18 years old and no longer a minor. Therefore, he could do what he wished, how he wished.

As Maupin started learning the tricks and ways of the pimp life, he continued to practice on women, especially the lady he delivered drugs too. However, this time in his life would soon come to an end because her significant other happened to be a police officer. One night, while Maupin roamed the streets, the officer caught up with him. He recognized Maupin as the person who had been sexually satisfying his woman, however, he had no proof. But this didn't stop the officer from finding a way to take Maupin off the streets.

As the officer frisked Maupin, he found a wad of cash. The officer questioned him about the cash because he knew all Maupin did was deliver medication to people. There was no way Maupin could make that amount of cash from his job. On top of that, the officer stated he found a key in Maupin's possession. Maupin responded that he had never seen that key before and the cash came from a game. The officer responded by taking Maupin in on charges of grand theft burglary.

The next morning, Mary came to see Maupin and couldn't believe what he had done. While Maupin tried to tell her that he had been set up, Mary refused to believe him. She said that the lady had already talked to the cops and said she hadn't seen Maupin in over a week. Mary told her son that she knew he stole the key and other things from her house. Again, he tried to tell her that it wasn't true, but she responded by stating that he needed prayer and was going to spend his life in prison if he kept going down the road he was on.

When Maupin found himself in front of the judge again, he was informed that none of his alibi's remembered seeing him that night. This made everyone believe that Maupin had, in fact, broken into her house and stolen a significant amount of money. After the lady took the stand to state that it was her key found in Maupin's possession and that he could have easily stolen it from her home while he made deliveries, he knew that there was no hope in getting out of a prison sentence. Maupin was right.

In his autobiography, *Pimp: The Story of My Life*, Maupin discusses how different the penitentiary was from the reformatory. He discussed how many cliques there were and how tough the other inmates were because most of the inmates he found himself around were murderers. Most were also significantly older than Maupin, who was still a teenager. While he didn't become close with many of the inmates, he did befriend inmates who had been pimps, including an older inmate. Through these inmates, Maupin began to learn more about the lifestyle and fell in love with what it held for people all over again. In fact, Maupin admits that at this time he became so infatuated with the lifestyle that he realized he didn't want to do anything else with his life. He wanted to become one of the greatest pimps anyone would ever know.

Maupin did whatever he could to stay out of trouble in the hope that his sentence would be reduced. This included getting a job in the laundry department. With this job, Maupin did everything he could to make sure his uniforms were clean and neat. One night, doing whatever he could to stay out of prison became even more important when the inmate he had befriended died in his cell. At that moment, Maupin made a vow to himself that he would never die alone in a prison cell. He would do whatever he could to live the life he wanted and stay out of prison.

Chapter 3

The Birth Of A Young Man Known As Cavanaugh Slim

When Maupin came back to Milwaukee, he immediately found a place on the streets where he could do the work he desired to do. Once he found his new place, Maupin's image quickly began to change. Instead of seeing himself as the 18-year-old he saw before he was sent to prison, he started to see himself as a great and powerful god.

At the same time, Maupin started to have terrible dreams. In these dreams, Maupin dressed the best by making sure his shoes were dazzling silver, his clothes were silk and often gold or rainbow colors. He made sure that he was clean and looked the part of the pimps he often saw as a child, especially Party Time. The women would follow his every step. He noticed how they would bow down to him like a god. It didn't take long for Maupin to completely fall in love with this lifestyle. However, the dreams would take a terrible turn as he would often murder the women who didn't listen to him. He would beat them until he saw them take their last breath. While the dreams bothered him, he started to notice that they also gave him some sort of pleasure upon waking up. However, soon another dream started to repeat. In this dream, Maupin would be told from a god-like figure to whip the evil out of the woman who had her back turned to him. He would do so and then come to realize that the person he was harming was his own mother. In his autobiography, Maupin wrote that he was never able to wake up from this dream until its end. Furthermore, he continued to have the dream until his mother passed away. He never truly understood the meaning of the dream but often felt it was because he knew that he was hurting her with his new lifestyle.

In order to cope with these nightmares, Maupin turned to drugs. He didn't just need to cope with the nightmares at night, but also during the day. They would haunt him to the point of depression. He never understood why these dreams came to him as he was not this type of man. At first, he started taking the medication he could snort from the drug store. He just needed something to get him a little high. However, he soon turned to street drugs, such as cocaine.

In reality, the dreams Maupin began having signaled that he had a difficult time between what he truly felt was morally right and the new lifestyle he was taking on. He felt guilt over the dreams, which would bring about guilt in his waking life. But, at the same time, Maupin had an incredibly strong desire to become a pimp. It was an internal struggle that Maupin would continue having until he finally decided to leave the world of pimping in his early 40s.

The dream of his mother also signaled the internal struggle he faced regarding her. He loved his mother, Maupin is open about that in his writings. However, he had always felt anger towards her because she chose to leave Henry. Maupin never wanted to leave the world that Henry gave him and Mary. In fact, for the rest of his life, Maupin would question what his life would have been like if his mother allowed him to stay with Henry instead of ripping him away from the home and love he had grown accustomed to.

At night, Maupin would find himself walking the streets and heading to the clubs which were full of pimps and prostitutes. It didn't take long for Maupin to find someone who remembered him. When he found them, he immediately asked about Party Time. He was then informed that Party Time was no longer around as he'd been busted and sent to prison, probably for the rest of his life.

With this news, Maupin decided that the next step for him to take was to find himself a woman he could pimp out. By surveying the scene, he found a young girl named Phyllis and upon asking his friend found out that she didn't have a pimp and was brand new on the scene, being only 18 years old. Maupin quickly found out that a lot of pimps didn't go for the young women because they considered them a lot of work. The more work they had to do, the less money they got paid. However, to Maupin, this seemed more like a test than anything else. After all, he found himself infatuated with her as he watched her go about the room. He also knew that he was younger than many of the other pimps on the scene as he was barely 20 years old. But, at the same time, Maupin knew he had to seem uninterested in her as she was interested in him. After all, he was taught you couldn't control the women if you didn't seem uninterested at first. He knew he had to make sure that she would do anything for him - at any time and without any trouble.

Maupin told Phyllis that his name was "Blood" and, eventually decided to follow her back to her place. By the time they left, Blood felt that he had tried to push her away enough and was happy with the fact she continued to try to get him. While they were at Phyllis' house, she did everything she could to get him to take his clothes off for her. However, he knew that he had to continue to play it cool. He had to be in charge or she would laugh at him and he would no longer have a chance at making her his girl. After trying to get him to listen to her, he demanded that she give him what he wanted. She immediately laughed at him and told him to get out. This is when part of Blood's nightmares came true.

He found himself standing up and knocking her down on the

floor. He looked at her as she fell on her stomach. He then started to kick her repeatedly. He didn't stop until his leg cramped up and he could no longer kick her. He then rolled her over and asked her if he had to kill her in order for her to become his whore. Through her tears and fear in her eyes, she shook her head and told him that he won. It was at this moment that he officially had his first woman as a pimp.

Off to Chicago

In the summer of 1942, Phyllis, Maupin, and possibly another girl left Wisconsin for the streets of Chicago, Illinois. Robert Maupin became a pimp known as Cavanaugh Slim. He didn't become synonymous with Iceberg Slim until 1965. Maupin's biographer, Just Gifford explains in his biography that Slim changed his name in his book as the name "Iceberg" matched his temperament better than "Cavanaugh." On top of this, Maupin saw Iceberg fitting after the assassination of Malcolm X.

Maupin was more determined to become one of the greatest pimps after he stepped foot onto the streets of Chicago. He told himself that he didn't care what he did, what other people did to him, or what happened; he was going to continue to pimp. Therefore, he dived right into the clubs where everyone in his career path went. He knew he needed to build his reputation and bring more women into his own personal village. He also knew he had to remember every rule and lesson that he learned in prison from the older pimps he met. He often repeated the lessons he learned and made sure he was following these lessons as he went about his business.

In a way, Robert Maupin and Cavanaugh Slim were two different people. When Maupin took on the name Cavanaugh Slim, he took on another persona. Cavanaugh Slim followed the unwritten rules of becoming a great pimp on the streets of Chicago. Slim quickly became known on the streets as having a temper yet able to remain calm when an emergency arose. In fact, this is how he got his name Cavanaugh Slim. He was not only known for being cold and cruel but he was also very tall and slim.

Once he entered Chicago, he explained his rules to his women. One of the rules was that he had to have a bottom woman, who was the main woman. She would control all the other women and make sure they followed the rules and completed their jobs as they were supposed to. Another rule was they had to treat him like their god. Slim learned how to get his women to do this psychologically. He had been told by other pimps during his last prison sentence that he needed to not only dress the part but also act the part. Like what he'd done with Phyllis when they first met, he had to make sure she knew who the boss was as soon as possible.

Slim would use various tactics in order to make sure his women followed his rules. While he was known to often beat women with wire hangers, he would often use other tactics first. One of his most popular tactics was psychological manipulation. In his autobiography, Maupin admitted that he was not a kind man and became very vicious. Later in his life, Maupin admitted that one of the biggest reasons he acted the way he did towards his women was because he needed to make them believe he was their god. He believed, as did many other pimps during Maupin's street days, if women saw their pimp as a god, they would be more likely to listen and follow the rules of the job.

Slim's Most Influential Hero

Slim spent a lot of time meeting with other notorious pimps of Chicago, such as Albert "Baby" Bell who became somewhat of a mentor for Slim. Bell was the one who taught Slim how to behave as a pimp. He told Slim that while he needed to learn everything he could about his women, they shouldn't know anything about him. He needed to remain mysterious and make sure to keep his emotions in check. In fact, Bell told Slim that he needed to conceal his emotions the best way he knew how. According to Bell, if women saw their pimp act emotionally, they would become harder to control. On top of this, showing emotion takes away the "god-like" image that great pimps were supposed to uphold. Basically, the more Slim was able to hide his emotions, the more successful he would become.

Slim admired Bell for many reasons. First, Bell was not only a notorious pimp in the Chicago area, but he had also lived that career for decades. Second, Slim loved the luxurious lifestyle that Bell lived due to his career. Not only did he have an ocelot, which is a wild cat, as a pet but he also drove a Duesenberg, which was a luxurious and expensive car at the time.

Slim admired Bell because he lived a life of fame on the streets of Chicago. Gossip columns would keep track of what Bell was doing. They would take his picture and write about the women he was with. This was something that Slim had never seen happen to a pimp before. He was in awe of the type of lifestyle that Bell lived. It was also the type of lifestyle he wanted. Therefore, Slim knew if he had any chance of making it like Bell, he needed to follow Bell's lead as much as possible.

Unfortunately, the type of person Bell was, was different from the type of person Maupin was. This only brought him deeper into the persona of Slim. Bell was notoriously known for his violence. In fact, everyone knew that Bell had killed at least four people. However, Slim didn't seem to mind the rumors and reputation that Bell had, no matter how bad he got. Slim wanted that fame and lifestyle. That was one of his main goals and he was going to hold onto that goal as long as possible. He was also going to do nearly everything in his power to reach the goal – at least at first.

Slowly, Slim started realizing that Bell's tactics and ways of pimping were different from all the other ways he had seen and learned throughout his life. While he was young, he never knew of Party Time being so vicious, or that he would have even wanted to. On top of this, all the pimps he had met while locked up in the Wisconsin prison system never spoke of such cruel and manipulative ways of controlling women and handling the system. While Slim quickly latched on to the idea of psychological manipulation, he simply couldn't accept the physical abuse – nearly torture – that he saw Bell put some women through. Bell was the one who taught Slim to use a wire hanger when he needed to.

Bell was also very quick to let Slim know that he had too many limitations, especially if he wanted to be the type of pimp he imagined. For example, Slim quickly learned that he smiled way too much. He also learned that he was just not "hard" enough to treat his women the way he should – or the way that Bell believed he should. Bell used his own psychological tactics to prove to Slim that he wasn't as tough as he believed he was. These tactics worked and Slim quickly realized that prison didn't harden him up like he first thought when he came to Chicago.

However, there was one psychological tactic that Bell knew would work to help harden Slim and that was using the anger Slim held for his own mother. Most of this anger, Slim tried to keep bottled up inside or would do whatever he could to ignore it. In reality, and as he admitted later in his life, Slim loved and cared for his mother deeply. As he stated in many interviews once he left the pimping world, he had a great mother who did everything she could in order to give him the best chance possible. He just didn't always accept what she was trying to do. He stated that most pimps on the streets didn't have much of a childhood and had been dumped on the streets by their mother. Slim had a different type of relationship than the majority of pimps during his youth. However, he was also young, angry, wanted a strong reputation as a notorious pimp, and felt hatred towards his mother for a few reasons.

Once Bell was able to reach into this anger that Slim held for his mother, Slim started to change a bit more. His personality started to harden as he started to become angrier. But the anger wasn't just for his mother, the anger was for every woman he saw. However, Bell was still not happy with the hardened personality. He would tell Slim that he wasn't cruel enough or he was "too soft." At first, this was increasingly challenging for Slim to hear because he wanted to follow Bell's lead. He wanted to become the nearly evil pimp that Bell was describing and telling him he needed to become. Slim soon started to realize that it might not be possible as he kept having an internal struggle between what was right and what Bell wanted him to do.

Bell's disappointment in Slim's personality was not the only concern Slim had once he truly started paying attention to the streets of Chicago. He also started to notice that the pimps in Chicago were vastly different than the pimps he knew in Wisconsin. Previously, Slim had become a strong and notorious pimp in Wisconsin. However, much of this was because most of the pimps on the streets of Milwaukee were weaker than the ones he met in Chicago. Slim started to realize that he had some really stiff competition and he quickly began to worry about being able to get near the top of the ladder.

Slim also realized that no matter how big his concerns were, they weren't going to help him make it to the top. He knew that if he continued to worry about every single word Bell said or how he didn't match up to his competition, he would never make it. Therefore, instead of drowning in his concerns, Slim worked to build up his stable of women. He sent Phyllis out on the street to find any girl that she thought would be good for his herd. In order to make them interested in being one of Slim's women, Phyllis was instructed to speak highly of him, talk about him like he was a god. She needed to discuss how he was not only smart that he was very sweet and that they would be well taken care of if they decided to go with her.

Slim also made his way onto the streets to look for women who peaked his interest. He didn't care if they had any experience in the pimping world or not. He would often bring them into his world by giving them cocaine, which had become his drug of choice on the streets. Once he noticed that they were high, he would start telling them of the amazing and luxurious life they could live if they became one of his women. He also told them that he would do anything to protect them. He would tell them if they were hurt by anyone, man or woman, that they should run back to him because he would be there for them. Of course, all the promises Slim made to these women were broken. He was in the business to make money for himself.

On top of that, he also put a woman out on the streets for up to 16 hours a day. They would go from one man to the other and fulfill the roles the men had paid for. This was a tactic that Bell taught Slim. He told Slim that he should never expect to have a woman for very long because his job was to send her out on the street for as long as possible and wear her out. Once she left, she was gone and another woman should be ready to immediately take her position. The same went for the main woman of the stable. Bell warned Slim that no woman would last very long and that it wasn't worth trying to keep them in longer than they should be. According to Bell, every woman had an expiration date and once this date came, it was time to let her go. Slim followed this instruction.

As time went on and Slim started to build up his stable, Bell continued to tell Slim everything that was wrong with what he was doing. He still smiled too much and he was still "too soft." While part of Slim had started to care a little less about what Bell was telling him, he also tried to figure out a solution. Soon, Slim started to realize that the more cocaine he did, the better he was able to fit into Bell's mold. Therefore, Slim started a daily schedule which involved an increasing amount of cocaine over the years. He would use cocaine while he was working and then make sure he got enough rest.

With his growing stable, he was able to focus more on rest and hiding out in his small hotel room while his herd continued to work long hours every day. However, with his increasing cocaine habit, Slim started to focus less on his appearance and started to become sloppier. However, when he was working, he did what he could to follow suit with the other pimps. Later in his life, Slim would admit that he never really did measure up to them. Part of it was that he had fallen so deep into his cocaine habit but the other part was he just didn't physically look the part. He stated he was never the best-looking man and he was starting to get older than many other pimps out there. Most of them were younger African American males. At the same time, he didn't hang out with them as often as they hung out with each other. Slim had his own daily routine, which included going to bed after a night out instead of continuing to hang out with other pimps until 8:00 in the morning.

Slim Finally Realizes His Dream

During the mid-1940s, Slim started to preach on the streets. He believed that this would be one way to gather women to join his flock, and he was not disappointed by the number of women who not only started to listen to his speeches but also follow him. In fact, when it came to the "red light district" on the south side of Chicago, Slim started to become a role model. People would go to listen to Slim not only because they were interested in joining his stable but also because they wanted to hear him speak. Whether what he said was true or not, he could speak in a way that not only made people listen but also made them believe he was highly intelligent.

In his speeches, he went from talking about what he could do for women if they joined his stable to how he was a broker due to the economics of sexual relations. He talked about how his lifestyle could make a person rich beyond their wildest imagination and he knew this to be true because he was his own proof. It was around this time that Slim finally met his goal as a pimp: he was near the top. In fact, he was considered one of the top among the new pimps on the streets of Chicago. Later in his life, Slim would discuss how it was at this moment he finally felt that he was free. That he was no longer tied down by the struggles of life. He felt like no one could touch him and no one could drag him down. He felt that he had truly been born for the pimp world.

Slim felt successful and like the ultimate god. He also felt free from America's race relations. The time was the 1940s and African Americans were struggling to make it in a white man's world for many reasons. They dealt with continuous racism, especially in the southern states. While Chicago was not southern, it was still known for its strict laws and regulations regarding African Americans. With his new found fame in the "red light district" neighborhood of Chicago, Slim felt that he could take on the world, including the white world. He really started to believe that he could be admired by both black and white people.

At the height of his career as a pimp, Slim had around 400 women working for him at any one time. He was living a life of luxury – the same life he had dreamed about. While he didn't have a stable home, as he often moved from one luxurious hotel room to the next, he didn't mind. He could afford it and this kept the cops and other people out of his hair. He bought all the flashy clothing and jewelry he wanted and started to snort more cocaine.

Eventually, Slim kept fewer women in his stable and more women in the lines waiting to come in. He started noticing that women were leaving at alarming rates. Some would only stay for a couple of nights while others might stay for a week. It became rare to see a woman there for longer than a month. But, none of this mattered to Slim anymore. He had made it to the top. What he was doing was working, therefore, he knew that he didn't need to worry about making any changes.

Above all, Slim realized that he could completely ignore the racist world he had lived in all his life. He didn't have to listen to white people telling him where he could and couldn't go. He didn't have to listen to them telling him what he could and couldn't do. He was able to stay in his luxurious hotel and receive everything he wanted by making other people get it for him. He no longer had to take the bumps and bruises as he could make other people take them for him. On top of this, it gave him added pleasure to know that the white men who would tell people of his race that they couldn't do certain things were driving around the streets of the "red light district" paying him for time with his women. As Slim would recall later in his life, there was nothing that fed his ego more than this realization.

Chapter 4

A Halt In Slim's Pimp Dream

America had just entered World War II, but Slim was able to avoid the draft because he refused to give his address to the military. At the same time, he was becoming sloppier with his stable. While he didn't seem to realize he was slowly losing control of his women, many others did, including his women. Phyllis was doing what she could in order to maintain control but she was also noticing her anger and frustration rising towards her boss.

Slim quickly learned that in order for him to make more money during the war, he could send his women to the army camps. Therefore, he started telling Phyllis that she and several other girls needed to go into Wisconsin and make money from the soldiers. While Phyllis complied, when she came back she had reached her breaking point. She had been completely humiliated by having to perform acts with United States servicemen. Therefore, when she returned with her herd, she began to challenge Slim and she knew exactly how

Phyllis went up to Slim, right in front of the other women and told Slim that without her, he would be a no one. She reminded him that before he found her, he was a no one and he didn't even know what he was doing. She had to help him learn. Then, she looked at Slim and told him that he was still incredibly inexperienced. This was the end for Slim. First, there was not one woman in his stable, including his main woman that could talk to him like that. He followed the book and rules of being a pimp and allowing that was not in the rule book. Second, she had verbally attacked Slim in front of his other women, this is not what his women did. They treated him like a god, as he believed he was a god to them. Slim knew, at that moment, that he had to make sure no other woman would react the way Phyllis had so he got up and punched her as hard as he could. Phyllis fell to the floor and immediately the other girls knew something was wrong. They quickly took her to the hospital to find out that Slim had broken her jaw.

Upon hearing this news, and realizing that he had lost control of his stable, Slim knew that his days on the Chicago streets as one of the top pimps were growing short. Therefore, he knew he had to do whatever he could to make a change. But, this did not include forgetting about his drug of choice, cocaine, which is one reason he was losing control as a pimp.

After other pimps heard what happened to Phyllis they gave him the advice that it was time to let her go, but he went about it the wrong way. They told him that in order to drive women away, he needed to make them want to leave. They often did this by making them feel crazy. Even some of the most ruthless pimps of Slim's time didn't drive their main woman away by beating her.

With this new advice, Slim did what he could to hit the streets and start building up his stable again. He did this by remembering he needed to remain calm and collected. Of course, being on the streets more meant that he had to start watching for the police. They continued to patrol the area and now, because Slim had made it to the top, many knew who he was. At the same time, his nightmares started to return at an alarming rate. Again, these nightmares, mainly ones about his mother, would carry on into his daily life.

Because of the nightmares, his lack of communication with his mother, and the threat of what he had built as a pimp falling to the ground, Slim started to look for a different drug to calm his nerves. He had taken so much cocaine for so long that it simply wasn't working as well as it should have. So, on a hot August day in 1944, Slim left the comforts of his hotel room and headed down the street to see if he could find some heroin to help him remain calm and collected.

Slim didn't realize that he had cops following his every move once they spotted him walking down the street. Once he was about to make the buy, the police arrested him and took him downtown for questioning and booking.

Leavenworth Federal Penitentiary

After booking, Slim was placed in the Cook County Jail. He found it worse than the reformatory or Wisconsin State Prison. The jail was more crowded than Slim could have imagined. In a small cell, which he stated in his autobiography was too small for two grown men, were eight men. Slim slept on the hard-concrete floor next to drug addicts who were going through withdrawals or coming down from a high. He remembered how there seemed to be someone puking at any given moment. He could barely stand the smell of the cell. There was very little space where Slim could be without having someone nearly puke all over him.

Of course, once Slim was booked, other laws he had been previously able to ignore caught up with him. While held in the Cook County Jail, they got him on charges of skipping out on the draft when he refused to update his address. While he was eventually going to go to prison, he was able to scrape up enough money for his bail.

After his release, Slim started to realize that everyone on the street knew that he was bound to be picked up and sent to prison over his charges. While he was currently out, his time was limited. He continued to find women who were willing to take chances with him, however, they never stayed very long. He started to struggle getting the money he needed to live because he was unable to keep more than a couple of women at once.

At the same time, more charges sprung up. Officials had found out that he was a pimp and had sent some of his women across state lines in order to perform sexual acts. Because this crossed the Illinois line into Wisconsin, it was now considered to be a federal case.

Slim was able to obtain help from a Milwaukee lawyer who advocated for African Americans. He told Slim that his best chance was to state he was guilty of his pimping charges as this would limit his stay in federal prison. Slim took his lawyer's advice and the judge sentence Slim to 18 months at Leavenworth Federal Penitentiary. About a week later, Slim boarded the train heading to Kansas to start his federal prison sentence.

This place was nothing like any other prison that Slim had ever seen or been in during his life. The first federal prison to be built in the United States, it could house about 2,500 people during Slim's day. On top of that, it was built like its own little community. Not only did it have a laundry, mechanic's area, and barbershop, but it also had a large hospital, farm, and a school.

This prison had strict rules which all prisoners had to follow, and Slim found them to be stricter than any other prison or jail he'd spent time in. One of the rules was that inmates weren't allowed to talk while they moved from one location to the next. When they sat down to eat, they all faced one direction and sat front to back. They were served by various waiters and were not allowed to speak or use hand signals during their meal times.

Security was also incredibly tight at Leavenworth. Instead of being checked once every hour, guards constantly walked up and down the hallways between the cells. There was no way anyone could look outside. Furthermore, no building had an exit that inmates were able to reach. And, in order to prevent any escape, there was a large chain fence which stood 40 feet tall and went well into the ground.

Once he was settled in Leavenworth, Slim met with countless professionals within his first couple of months. He spoke with ministers, doctors, prison officials, and even psychiatrists. On top of this, he was given a clean bill of health from a medical doctor, however the dentist found that he didn't have good teeth. They also gave him an I.Q. test, which showed Slim to have average intelligence. However, through all his interviews with these professionals, Slim continued to bend the truth, hide parts of his past, or lie. For example, instead of telling his psychiatrist that he had been a pimp for years, he told the doctor that he had been a salesman, nightclub dancer, singer, magician, and hotel clerk. However, he was unable to make his psychiatrist believe him. The doctor had seen his record and knew that he was a pimp and had been a pimp since he was 17 years old.

Even in a strict facility like Leavenworth State Penitentiary, Slim continued to keep women working for him on the streets of Chicago. He still owed people money, including his stepfather who he had borrowed money from in order to make bail. Slim figured if he continued to do what he could to manage women on the outside, he could pay off his stepfather and possibly have some money when he got out of Leavenworth.

But, every lie that Slim told would eventually catch up with him and he would find himself in further legal trouble. When this happened, he admitted to some of his lies but tried to manipulate by stating he didn't understand everything that had been asked. Because of his lies and manipulation, the board told him that he would not be up for an early release as this privilege had now been revoked. He would also remain in quarantine for some time.

In fact, Slim didn't get out of quarantine until July of 1945. When he was placed in general population, he was given the basics of a Bible, mirror, comb, brush, hand soap, blanket, cup, and towel. Because Leavenworth was segregated, Slim was held with African Americans, who were mainly drug dealers and pimps.

Even though Leavenworth had very strict rules, this didn't stop other inmates from beating on each other. The worst threat to African Americans was from the Southern cons. They couldn't stand African Americans and hated each and every one of them. In his later life, Slim discussed how much violence he saw break out because of the attacks African Americans faced at the hands of the Southern cons.

Chapter 5

Back On The Fast Track

Not even Leavenworth Federal Prison could keep Slim from going back to his pimping ways. He saw his release from there in 1947 and immediately headed back to his mother's house. However, he would only stay about a week with her and her husband before looking for a cheap place to rent. While he didn't have too many women in his stable, he had a few, and this was enough to get his career back up and running.

Upon his return, Slim had to spend time figuring out ways to build his stable back up. He had no stable because he had no women. He needed to go back out there and find himself someone who would be able to help build up his stable. He knew that there wouldn't be a lot of women who would want to work for him because of his reputation. Everyone knew he had just gotten out of federal prison. On top of that, most of the main pimps he hung out with were now locked up or had very few women of their own. He noticed that some men had three women while others only had one.

However, Slim had one big problem before he could really go

out there and start his pimp lifestyle again. He didn't have any of the right supplies. He wasn't looking his greatest and on top of this, he didn't have any fancy clothes or shoes. He didn't have any big, shiny jewelry to show off to potential women who were looking for a man and money. In order to get back into the game, he needed to fit the part. However, he also didn't know how he could come up with the money for the supplies he needed without having a woman to pimp out.

After debating what to do, he decided to just go out there and see if he could find himself a woman who would work for him. So, he started hitting his old clubs again and quickly ran into someone who was down and out on his luck like he was. Red Eye was the man's name and he had gotten out of jail a little before Slim did. They bonded at the club over their stories and how they craved the right women for their stables. At this point, they didn't just want to find someone to pimp out, they also wanted to find someone for themselves.

While they bonded, they discussed how they could even find women and work together. They talked about ways that they could make better money doing this. This is when Red Eye came up with a different plan. One which involved finding one of the richest women in the neighborhood and acting as police in order to get the money they wanted. While Slim agreed with the plan at the club, he became nervous about the whole deal later that night. In his autobiography, he wrote about how he stayed up most of the night trying to find another way to make money. He even thought of finding any woman that he could take the time to turn into the right kind of woman to pimp out. He thought that if he had someone, he would at least be able to make enough money to get by until he had her trained for her new career. However, he also knew the business better now than he had before and knew that this rarely worked. People just didn't pay for those types of women. Therefore, against his better judgment, Slim decided that Red Eye's was the best plan. So, he met Red Eye the next night in order to enact their plan.

The plan was to act as police, pretend to arrest her and bring her back to the van that one of Red Eye's friends was driving. Red Eye knew that Slim would be the best one to do most of the talking because he was known to be a good actor. Once they saw her walking into the alley towards her car, Slim and Red Eye made their move. Slim stopped her and stated that he was a police officer, even showing her a badge, and asked her what she was doing walking alone in the alley so late at night. The woman told him that her name was Gloria Jones and that he better watch out because her husband was good friends with the deputy sheriff. While Slim became a bit more nervous at this point, he was able to stick to the plan. He told her that her real name was Mavis Sims and, as she struggled, they brought her to the van.

Once they were back in the van, Red Eye's friend drove off. While in the van, Mavis told the men she knew they weren't cops. After Red Eye got hold of the gun that Mavis had by frisking her, they started to look for cash. It took Slim a minute to remember that his women used to hide their cash near their private area. This is when things took a turn for the worst, especially for Mavis. She refused to give in to Red Eye, who was telling her to allow him to search her. After her refusal, Red Eye punched her in the face and then the stomach to make her give in to his demands. After he searched her, the men were able to split a few thousand dollars between them. As a bonus, Red Eye found Mavis' stash of drugs.

Now, instead of following the life of a pimp in order to make money, Slim was robbing people and Red Eye was very ruthless about it. However, this career wouldn't last long for Slim as not even a week later, they would pick someone who didn't have cash and get caught by the police. As they were trying to search the man, a police car drove up and realized what was going on. While Red Eye's friend got away, Slim and Red Eye were pulled out of the van by the police officers.

It's Gonna Be A Jailbreak

By this time, Slim had a record. He had not only spent time in jail twice in Wisconsin but had also been sent to Leavenworth Federal Penitentiary. There was no way that he was going to get off of anything. He was heading back to prison and he knew it. That was until his lawyer advised both him and Red Eye to take a deal. If they pleaded guilty, he stated that instead of prison, they would end up in a workhouse. The lawyer was correct. At their sentencing, the judge ordered both Slim and Red Eye to a workhouse for a year. Unfortunately, Slim would find the workhouse to be worse than any prison he had ever been in.

Of course, Slim hadn't committed the right type of crime in order to be treated like a person in the workhouse. From his observations, he noticed that only the top cons were treated with any sort of decency. On top of this, the place was filthy. In fact, Slim had never seen a place as filthy as the workhouse, including the time he was crammed into a cell at Cook County Jail.

It didn't even take a week for Slim to start thinking about different ways to escape. It even got to the point where he didn't care if he died trying. He was becoming increasingly desperate to get out of the workhouse and was willing to try anything. While at first none of the ideas Slim thought of would work out, as he tried to formulate the plan in his head he happened to stumble on the best way by accident one night.

Unlike his last stint at Leavenworth, the guard who did the count at the end of the day didn't make the inmates stand in front of their cell doors. Slim realized this one night when he slept through the count. He then decided to test the guard to see how much of him the guard had to see in order to count him. Once he noted that as long as the guard saw his back and legs he'd count him, Slim started to put a real plan into action.

He began to collect all the materials he would need to make the guard believe he was sleeping in his bunk so he had time to escape and be long gone before the guard even noticed he was missing. As Slim worked on other parts of his plan, such as when to leave, he also thought about how he could talk his cellmate into helping him. He needed his cellmate to put the dummy on his bed once he escaped in order to give him time to run off to minimize the risk of being caught. After some bribing, which including telling the young 18-year-old who was in awe of Slim's pimp lifestyle, that he would teach him how to pimp when he got out of the workhouse, the cellmate agreed to the plan.

On the day of his escape, Slim worked as normal and then while the inmates were lined up and walking towards the kitchen for supper, he slipped into an open storage area. Once the storage room locked, he waited for the whistle to blow. The guards would blow a whistle after the end of day count to let everyone know that all inmates were accounted for. In order for this plan to work, Slim's cellmate had to place the dummy on the bed correctly. Slim couldn't believe it when the whistle blew as he was sure that the guards had noticed it was just a dummy on his bed and not him. He stated in his autobiography that hearing that whistle blow brought tears to his eyes.

After hearing the whistle, Slim made his escape. He snuck out of the building through a window and then climbed up the wall using his hands, feet, and stomach. Unfortunately, the escape wouldn't end without pain as when Slim was at the top of the wall, he fell to the ground. Once he was able to stand, he limped his way towards Indiana. He needed to get to his aunt's house, about 30 miles away.

Back Into The Game

Once Slim got to his aunt's house, she fixed up his leg and her husband gave him some clothes. On Slim's way out the door about a week later, his aunt and uncle gave him about $50. He headed straight to find the areas where the pimps hung out. Within a few days, he found himself another woman. Together, they started heading north. Slim quickly realized that his new woman, whose name was Helen, was great at stealing. This is one of the ways they were able to make their way from Indiana into Iowa and then into Minnesota.

However, it didn't take Helen and Slim long to see they wouldn't be able to work together very long. Helen was tougher than a lot of other girls Slim had been with and he found himself a bit out of the loop in the pimp world. As he traveled and worked with Helen, he realized that he didn't really know as much as he thought.

After Helen and Slim got into a fight, which ended up with her stabbing him, he decided the best course of action was for him to learn her stealing technique. He would then be able to get rid of her and find other women who he could train to do the same thing. Because Slim had learned how to psychologically manipulate people, he was able to get Helen to explain her technique pretty quickly. Slim listened well so he would be able to train his future women.

Off To Detroit

It didn't take long for Helen to get busted, which made Slim's job of getting rid of her easier. However, he also knew that he had to get out of town because people could come after him next. After discussing his options with other pimps he'd started to trust, he learned that Detroit, Michigan, was the place to go for pimps. Therefore, he took the last of his cash and headed to Michigan.

It didn't take Slim long to get back into the game and his old ways in Detroit, because the women weren't like the women from Chicago. They weren't as smart and they believed the things Slim told them easier than any women he had known before. The first woman he picked up on Detroit's streets was a woman named Rachel. At the time, she had yet to turn 18 years old, but she was ready for the world Slim had promised her.

After Rachel, he continued to find other women. However, he didn't work as fast as he did back on the streets of Chicago. He wasn't aiming for the highest number of women he could. Instead, he was aiming for women who would get the job done and give him the money he needed. It didn't take long, only about three months, for Slim to start living the life of luxury he adored once again. Once he was able to start playing the part of the sharp, clean, and rich pimp, more women started to join his stable.

Slim's Stable Moves

After Slim got back in the game, he learned of a small town in Ohio that grabbed his attention. He started thinking that he could leave Detroit and open a couple of houses there. His ego was starting to return as he began to get back into his groove with five women who would do anything for him. On top of that, Slim felt that it was time to move on, especially since Ohio would give him better business than Detroit.

Therefore, Slim decided to move his stables. He traveled to Ohio and got in touch with a couple of people who would open doors for him. Not long after he got set up in Ohio, he went back to get his women. They all piled into Slim's car and headed to Ohio. It wasn't long after that Slim found out the area he'd stayed in in Detroit was nearly shut down by the police. Slim thought himself very lucky when he heard this news. Not only was he a pimp but he was a wanted for running away from the workhouse.

In Ohio, Slim was on cloud nine. However, one night his world came crashing down when one of his women, Serena, tried to stab him with an ice pick. Later, he went to Serena's place with a gun and told her that anyone who tried to kill him, including his own mother, would be killed. But, when it came time to follow through with the threat, Slim couldn't do it.

A few hours later, as he walked into Rachel's place with the rest of his women, they saw Serena standing across the room with the ice pick. Slim drew his gun and once again warned her that if she tried anything, he would kill her. She told him she no longer cared and ran for them, which is when Slim shot her in the chest. However, this didn't kill her. While he had the chance to shoot her in the head, he couldn't bring himself to do it. Serena escaped.

The rest of them knew that they had very little time to get out of that area. Therefore, they left everything they owned and ran to Slim's car. He drove himself and his four remaining women towards his mother's house. He hadn't seen her in years but knew that it was one place he could go. Slim was honest with his mother and told her what happened between him and Serena. In order to help her son, Mary went down to Ohio to gather their belongings. She also stopped at the hospital were Serena was recovering. During their meeting, Serena told Mary that she was sorry for what had happened and if Slim took her back, she wouldn't press charges. However, Slim refused. He stated in his autobiography that he knew if he went back to Ohio, she would kill him.

Slim wouldn't stay in his old stomping grounds very long. While he liked being close to his mother, he couldn't stay there because everyone knew him. Therefore, he formulated a plan and decided to return to Ohio. Once he was there, he set up a house in both Cleveland and Toledo and, once again, began to see the cash roll in. However, Slim's luck wouldn't hold much longer.

His main girl, Rachel, was on every pimp's list. She was always hearing about offers for her from other pimps and Slim knew he couldn't lose someone like Rachel. He knew how losing her would end his career as a pimp. In fact, he wouldn't be able to pimp in any of the surrounding states because they would all hear that he lost his main girl to another pimp. On top of that, he knew that if Rachel was given the chance, she would let the Federal investigators know where he was and he would be busted. Therefore, he worked hard and fast to try to come up with a plan to make sure Rachel stayed with him. While, the whole time he kept telling himself he had to remain cool and collected.

In order to keep Rachel by his side, Slim thought of a hoax. He contacted Rachel and told her she had work to do in a nearby town. He drove her there but before she headed up to the hotel room, Slim dropped cooking oil on her hand but told her it was Chloral Hydrate, which would knock the man out so she could search his room for cash. Not long after, Rachel came down to get Slim because the man was out but she couldn't find any cash. He followed her up there and told her that he believed the man was dead. Rachel started to panic. She had talked to the desk attendant and a lot of people had seen her. She knew murder was a lot worse than theft.

Slim told her to calm down and said he would take care of it. He then told her to hide in the closet while he called the doctor. However, this doctor was a friend of Slim's and only playing a doctor; just like the man lying on the floor was only pretending to be dead. Once Slim's doctor friend came in, he told Slim that he needed to call the police because the man had passed away. Slim then talked to the doctor and, following the plan, the doctor agreed that he would not tell the police that Slim or Rachel were there. At that moment, Slim grabbed Rachel from the closet and the two drove back to Rachel's place.

On the drive home, Slim knew that Rachel had no choice but to stay with him. Especially when he told her that the only way to keep her secret safe was to stay with him for the rest of his life.

It didn't take long after this move for Slim to realize that Cleveland had started buzzing with police. Therefore, Slim started to hide at his place. He was a fugitive and he knew that the second he was caught; his freedom would be gone. In his autobiography, Slim admits that he hardly left his place for over a year due to the fear of getting arrested.

History Catches Up To Slim

As Slim continued to pimp in Ohio, he started to realize that he was getting older than most of the pimps out there. However, this wasn't the only thing catching up to Slim. One night, as he hung out around the town, Slim ran into someone who knew him from his Chicago days. As they started talking, Slim was informed that this man now had Phyllis and she was passed out up in her room. Once he found out it really was Phyllis, Slim knew he had to leave the area. He knew that Phyllis would be one of the first people to call the police and let them know where he was hiding out. Slim knew that Phyllis had heard he'd escaped from the workhouse. Therefore, Slim took the next flight out to Los Angeles, California, where his mother and her new husband had moved.

However, Slim only stayed in California a few months. He refused to move his women out there because it would be bad for his career. Therefore, they stayed in Ohio and Rachel would send him money. After his stay in California, Slim decided to head up to Seattle, Washington.

It was in Seattle that Slim ran into an old friend. The two started to reminisce about the old days and both started to get the urge to start pimping in Seattle. From there, it didn't take long for Slim to send his women to other areas. This would prove to be a mistake as he sent one woman, Stacy, to a small area in Montana. Slim's friend warned him that this was a bad idea but Slim didn't listen.

Slim would go to Montana to meet with Stacy every few months. During one visit, Stacy informed him that another man had been trying to take her away. It wasn't long after this that the police knocked on their hotel room door. Slim had used a fake name at the register but the police knew "his type." They knew that he was a pimp and Stacy was his woman. The police officers told them to leave immediately. However, because the train only left once a day and there was a blizzard, Slim and Stacy were unable to leave.

The next day, the Chief of Police came to the door. Once again, Slim tried to play cool with the chief, who asked if the two were married. Slim told him that they had gotten married three years ago, but the chief refused to believe him. He took them down to the station and upon searching for Slim's record, found out that he was a fugitive and wanted for escaping from the workhouse.

While Stacy was released, Slim was sent back to the workhouse he had escaped from thirteen years before. Luckily for Slim, he only had to live eleven months in the workhouse. But, he knew from the beginning that he would be watched like a hawk.

While Slim was in the workhouse, he kept in touch with his

mother, Stacy, and Rachel. He knew his mother was sick and dying, so he worried about her a lot. In fact, his last few letters from her he could barely read her writing. Soon, she became bedridden and the only information he received about her was from her friends. After a few months, both Rachel and Stacy left Slim's life. Rachel found out about the hoax that Slim and a couple of his friends had played on her in order to get her to stay with Slim. Stacy got pregnant and started a life with one of her old pimps. Soon, Slim wasn't getting any kind of letters or cash from Stacy. On top of everything else, Slim wasn't looking too good himself. He was getting sick often and losing a lot of weight.

Slim's Decision

During the middle of his seventh month, Slim received some bad news about Party Time. He had gotten mixed up with someone who had mixed some drugs with battery acid. Slim was heartbroken at the news and stayed up that whole night thinking about his days with Party Time, his career as a pimp, and his struggle with drugs. It was at that moment when he decided that it was time to make a change. In that dark and dirty cell, Slim decided that he was finally done with his pimping lifestyle. He would find another way to make money. Furthermore, he would stop taking drugs and follow the law so he never had to end up in a jail cell again.

Night after night, Slim laid in bed awake, thinking about how much he'd wasted his life. He thought about how he could have stayed in college and became a doctor. He thought about how he had spent his life and the heartache he had caused his mother during all those years. This is what really started to get Slim thinking about fighting for an early release. He knew he had to get out before his mother passed away. He needed to get to her to tell her that he did love her, to tell her that he was truly sorry, and to tell her that he was finally going to turn his life around.

Slim tried on more than one occasion to get out of his sentence early. He met up with the board for an interview on a couple of occasions, one happening within his tenth month, just a few weeks before his legal discharge date. However, neither of these interviews would end in Slim's favor. Upon Slim's release, he was sent fare from one of his mother's friends so he could make it to California.

Chapter 6

To Turn In A Different Direction

Slim decided that in order to leave his past behind him, he needed to change his name. However, he didn't want to take the last name of Maupin again as this reminded him of the father who had left him and his mother. Therefore, he took the name of Beck, which had been the last name of one of his mother's husbands. This meant that he was no longer Slim, he was Robert Beck.

While Beck tried to get back on his feet, he struggled with memories from his time in solitary confinement in the workhouse. When it came to his years in various prisons, the last place was the worst place for Beck. He could never fully shake the horrifying memories of violence there. In fact, he continued to struggle with the memories until the day he passed away.

Unfortunately, Beck didn't just struggle to get back on his feet because of haunting visions from the workhouse. The year was 1962 and segregation in California was still prevalent. Even though it wasn't as bad as some areas in the United States, Slim still struggled finding a job and a place to live. Of course, this was also because of his criminal past. However, Beck refused to let these struggles get to him. He refused to go back to the streets; back to the drugs and the life of a pimp. He had made a promise to his mother that he would not go back to his old ways. He was bound and determined that he would not disappoint her anymore as she clung to life.

To Find A Wife

Therefore, Beck did whatever he could to get back on his feet. He was able to secure a low-wage job which helped with his mother's rent. At the same time, he also focused on making good another promise, to show his mother that he had changed and was going to start a family. Since Beck had moved in with his mother, she'd told him she wanted to see him happy with a family. She wanted him to get married and experience being a father. She wanted to see this before the Lord took her home.

Beck never truly opened up about his worries of finding a wife to his mother as he didn't want Mary to learn how he had treated women during his days as Slim. However, he was not going to give up on his mother's wish either. Beck's problem was that he really only knew how to stalk and control women. He didn't know how to date. In fact, he had never really dated except for his early teenage years. He was now in his 40s and had lived over two decades as a pimp.

As Beck worked through his problem, he realized that he could take some of the skills he'd learned during his years as Slim and bring them into the dating scene. Therefore, he cleaned himself up and found his best suit. He then went out, stopping at random diners and restaurants in search of a woman that could become his wife. This is when he met a young woman named Betty Shue (sometimes written as Shew).

Betty was from Austin, Texas and had moved to Los Angeles, California in search of an adventure. Born in 1936, Betty was much younger than Beck but he didn't mind. Once he heard her story of her difficult start in Los Angeles, including when she found her birth father who then tried to rape her once she got to the city, Beck knew that she was in need of not only a friend but someone to protect her. If there was one thing Beck knew how to do, it was make a woman see that she needed him.

Betty was also young and naive. She quickly noticed that Beck looked clean and was always dressed in a nice suit. At the time, she had no idea that this suit was from his days as a pimp. Instead, she believed that he was a lawyer or a doctor.

Betty struggled to learn much about Beck, but she also knew that she was starting to like him and she believed that he also liked her. Beck continued to drive to the diner where Betty worked to eat lunch. As he ate, he would say very little but he always told her that he would come back the next day to see her. As the days went on, Betty started to find herself looking for his car and waiting for his visit.

Only a few days after they first met, Beck asked Betty if she would be interested in going somewhere else. He wanted to take her someplace where they could get some soul food. Betty agreed and the pair arranged their first date. Betty was in her mid-20s and had been on a few dates. Beck was in his mid-40s and had never been on an official date before. However, he was determined to make Betty his wife for his mother.

On their first date, Beck arrived with a gift for Betty. While she was cautious at first, she accepted the large box and found a nice little dress. While she felt excited, she was also a bit embarrassed. No one had given her such a nice gift before and she was unsure how to act. Her uneasiness about the dress intensified as she tried it on and realized it was a perfect fit. She couldn't understand how a man who had just met her about a week before would know what size of dress she would wear. She continued to try to figure out who this man truly was as the date went on.

The date would take a turn when Betty started feeling intense pain and got sick in Beck's car. Instead of taking her home, Beck took her to the Emergency Room where they found out that Betty was four months pregnant and her body was trying to abort the baby. Betty couldn't believe the news as she hadn't shown any signs of pregnancy. She hadn't even missed her period. She became distraught and wondered how she would be able to take care of herself. The doctors told Betty that if she wanted to have the baby, she would have to remain in bed until the birth. When Beck came into Betty's room, she cried and told him that she didn't know what to do. Beck told her that it would be okay, he would bring her back to his mother's apartment and take care of her and his mother.

However, Mary was still unsure that her son really had changed. She feared that instead of taking care of Betty, he wanted to get her ready for the streets. Mary became so fearful of this idea, especially knowing there was a baby on the way, that she snuck into Betty's room once to tell her to run away. She told Betty that she loved her son, but he wasn't any good. Betty didn't understand what Mary meant, so she asked Beck about it, but he refused to tell her anything. He simply told her that it wasn't the time to explain his past. She needed to focus on keeping herself and her baby healthy. Later in his life, Beck would admit that he never really loved Betty. He simply needed to make sure he had a wife before his mother died because he wanted her to see her wish had come true. He also knew that Mary wouldn't be around much longer and this meant he would need to have someone in his life. After all, there were things he needed a woman to do in his life, such as cooking and cleaning.

Betty didn't get to know Mary very well as she passed away a couple of months after Betty came to live with the family. While Betty knew that Beck would take his mother's death hard, even though he knew it was coming, she didn't realize how difficult the time would be for him. While she didn't understand his strong reaction at the time, she later realized why he took the death so hard. It was due to all the trouble he felt had been caused by his mother for all those years. Later in her life, Betty stated, "...Never in my life seen anybody suffer the way he did...I never saw such love of a parent as he had for his mother. And I never saw such guilt in a child for what he had done to his mother."

Another New Beginning

After the death of Mary, life didn't get any easier for the couple. Beck barely had time to make any money working because he had been busy taking care of his mother and Betty. While Betty was doing better, she still needed to remain on bed rest for the baby. Beck wasn't sure what type of work he could find because all he knew was how to pimp. The couple ended up moving into a cheaper place because they could no longer afford the rent on his mother's two-bedroom apartment.

Beck did everything he could to make Betty comfortable and happy. He even looked for a different apartment when she complained that the one they were living in was too depressing for her. Fortunately, Beck had accepted a job as an exterminator, so they were financially able to move to a little bit better place. After Beck had learned a little about the extermination business, he decided to work on establishing his own business. He learned what type of chemicals were needed and then started to go door to door asking people if they were in need of his services.

Beck dug into his skills as a pimp when he started his business. He knew how to make something out of nothing and he knew the type of person people liked to do business with. He knew that he could be as personable as he needed to be in order to get them to accept his services and earn some money. However, this doesn't mean that the business Beck started was a legal business. Beck knew that he couldn't just knock on people's doors and be a nobody with chemicals willing to exterminate in and around their home. He needed to show that he had a business. Therefore, he created a fake business, with a fictional person as the owner and one of his friends as the sales representative.

For a while, Beck's fake company and skill at making people believe they needed his services, even if they didn't have a bug infestation, worked well. The couple was able to make rent and have enough money left over for groceries. Unfortunately, Betty was about to give birth and they had nothing for the baby. On top of this, Beck knew that they wouldn't be able to afford anything the baby needed as he barely made enough money for their food. Beck quickly started thinking about other ways he could make money without having to go back to the streets.

Beck thought he'd found the best solution when he met a partially paralyzed woman named Rosa, who needed some help at home. As Beck and Rosa started talking, they came up with the idea that Beck and Betty would move into her spare bedroom and instead of paying rent, Betty would help Rosa with the household chores that needed to be done. While Beck thought this was a great idea, Betty was unsure of the whole situation. She didn't have a good feeling about it. However, Betty also saw no choice as the baby was coming soon and they didn't have enough money. Therefore, Betty agreed and the couple moved in with Rosa.

What Beck didn't know is that Rosa would be difficult to live with and that she was an alcoholic. It didn't take long for Betty to realize that this was a bad move. Betty was unable to get the rest she needed because Rosa would throw parties late into the night. On top of this, Betty was performing tasks that she felt was putting her baby in danger. She was not only doing the cleaning, but she was also giving Rosa baths. It only took Betty a couple of weeks before she told Beck that they couldn't stay there any longer.

At first, Beck thought Betty was just being hormonal or overdramatic. However, Betty's frustration continued to grow and soon she was telling him that if she continued to do this work, she would either harm herself or Rosa. It was at this point that Beck knew the couple needed to leave so he found a different apartment.

Beck Becomes A Father

With the baby coming in less than a month, Beck went back to exterminating. He didn't know how the couple would make it, but he knew this would give them some money. On June 24, 1963, Robin made his way into the world and Beck loved his new role as a father. As the days went on, Beck started to realize how lucky he was. It was very unusual for a pimp to experience fatherhood. At the same time, Beck knew nothing about raising children. He didn't know how to be a father. His career as a pimp didn't teach him anything about fatherhood and the only true father he felt he ever had was Henry.

But the last thing Beck was going to do was give up on his child. Even though Robin was the product of a previous relationship of Betty's, Beck promised Betty that he would raise him like his own son and this is what Beck was determined to do. It also didn't take long for the couple to grow their family. Less than two years after Robin made his way into the world, their first daughter, Camille, joined the family on September 10, 1964. Later in his life, Beck admitted that he often struggled with parts of fatherhood, and much of this had to do with his lifestyle as a pimp. He just couldn't handle some of the things most fathers could, such as their child kissing them on the cheek or picking up his children.

Beck also let his fears of a racially segregated world get in the way of him playing with his children. Betty was white and so was their son, Robin. However, their daughter was mixed. This worried Beck because he knew that children who were the product of interracial relationships often dealt with discrimination. Beck knew he had a violent temper and while he worked hard to control his temper with and around his children, he was sure he wouldn't be able to control it if someone harmed his children. In fact, he became adamant that he would kill someone who harmed one of his children. Therefore, he felt that it was best if he sat back when his family was out in public. After all, people were more likely to verbally attack the family if they saw Beck with them. They would leave Betty and the kids alone until they saw an African American male with a white female.

On top of this, with the Civil Rights Movement, Beck feared more for his family's safety. He also feared the riots that were breaking out across the country. While Beck wanted to go out there and be a part of the Civil Rights Movement, he didn't want any harm to come to his family. He also didn't want to end up going back to jail. They had two kids and he knew that going to jail would just make the family's struggles worse. Therefore, he stayed away from any of the riots and the Civil Rights Movement events until he had no other choice.

During August of 1965, the Watts riots took place on the streets of Los Angeles. Beck's fear for his family's safety escalated when he saw people walking up and down the street right outside their apartment window with weapons. They were breaking into businesses and causing all types of damage around the neighborhood. In order to protect his family the best he could, Beck told Betty to lock her and the kids into the back bedroom. They were not to come out until she heard his voice, no matter what happened. Even though the riots ended and nothing happened to the family, it took Beck a long time before he felt comfortable enough taking them out of their apartment. A few years later, the couple would be blessed with another daughter, Misty.

Chapter 7

Writing, Music, and Films

It was not long after the riots when Beck finally felt it was time to open up to Betty about his past. However, the reason for this happened nearly by accident. He started telling her stories about his days as a pimp because it helped him relax after a long day exterminating bugs and rats. As time went on, Betty started to enjoy listening to the stories. Once he got home, she would get the children ready for bed and then sit down with him and listen to whatever story he decided to tell. It wasn't always the stories that Betty enjoyed hearing, it was the way Beck told the stories.

Betty found Beck to be an amazing storyteller and she knew that he had lived a life that many people would be interested in hearing about. After all, if she was part of his family and found these stories to be fascinating, there was going to be hundreds if not thousands of other people who would feel the same way. This is when Betty came up with the idea for Beck to publish his stories.

At first, he wasn't sure that it was something he wanted to do.

He didn't write down his stories, he told them to her so he could relax at the end of the day. In a sense, it helped him unwind so he would be able to sleep better. However, one night as Beck started telling her stories, Betty grabbed a notebook and started writing the story down. After he'd finished the story, Betty showed him his story written on paper. At first, Beck was still skeptical about the whole situation. He couldn't write the stories down himself. This is when Betty said that she knew how to type and they could work on it together.

It didn't take long for Beck to start feeling a bit more comfortable with the idea. After all, it would be another way for them to make money. The money factor became even more important when the couple's third daughter, Melody, came home in the fall of 1965.

Beck finally agreed to the book idea when he realized that it would give him something to take the place of pimping. While he was no longer a pimp and would never dream of returning to that type of life, he also knew that there was a piece of it he missed. He believed the book would help fill this hole. Therefore, after the kids were in bed, Beck would tell Betty a story and she would put it on paper. While it took a while, they eventually started to see the book come together.

Once the book was complete, Beck couldn't believe what they had done. He knew that this was a book like no other book on the shelves. He also knew that this book would open the world to the underground world of pimping. It was his truth, full of harsh realities which could be considered pornographic at times. It was full of drugs, violence, and the struggles of making it as one of the top pimps.

In Need Of A Publisher

With the book pretty much completed, Beck started looking for a publisher. Both Beck and Betty believed that the book was going to sell millions and hoped it would make the best-sellers list. However, they also knew that because of the type of book it was, and the fact that Beck was African American, it would be difficult to find a publisher and get the book on the shelves. This is why when Beck found someone interested, a lot quicker than he anticipated, he became extremely excited. However, it also didn't take Beck long to realize that he shouldn't get too excited.

The man that Beck trusted to help him finish the book and find a publisher was a professor at a local college. Both men were impressed with the other and Beck believed that the professor had great credentials for the type of work Beck needed. However, as they started working together, Beck quickly realized that there was something strange about the professor. As time went on, Beck started to trust him less and less.

One of the first things that stuck out to Beck was that the professor hung out with white people who lived luxurious lifestyles. Beck started wondering why someone like that would want to help him, an African American who was a former pimp. Whether this concern was a result of the segregation Beck faced in his life or because of some other reason remains unknown. However, for the majority of his life, Beck had been weary of people like the professor. They usually couldn't find the time during their day to help someone like him. Therefore, Beck kept questioning why the professor would want to help him. But, at the same time, Beck wanted to get his book published. He continued to push his worries out his mind and focus more on the task at hand.

When it came time for Beck to sign the contract that the professor's lawyer had written up, Beck became even more suspicious. Later in his life, Beck admitted that part of this had to do with the fact he had just been released from jail a few years early and was still very cautious and uneasy about being an American citizen. At the same time, the Civil Rights Movement was still going strong. And while Beck wasn't highly educated, he knew when someone was trying to take advantage of him. Therefore, he made sure to read the contract very closely.

As Beck read, he saw that their agreement of splitting

royalties 50/50 was in there, however, there were also pieces of the contract that didn't sit right with him. In the contract was a clause that basically took all rights away from Beck. After reading this, he refused to sign the contract and decided to end his relationship with the professor. Of course, the professor's lawyer kept pressuring Beck, but he refused to give in. Even the many letters Beck received from the lawyer, one threatening that the professor was going to write and publish the book before him, didn't shake Beck enough to sign the contract.

As Beck and Betty kept working on the book, Beck decided to take his chances at Holloway House. He walked into the offices with a few pages from the book and asked one of the editors to read it. Milton Sickle was the editor who read the pages of Beck's autobiography and fell in love with the book. Malcolm X's autobiography had just come out and Sickle knew that Beck's book could be a hit as well. Sickle refused to let Beck leave without signing a contract, which he did. Upon signing the contract, Beck received a $1,500 advance and would receive $0.04 per book in royalties. Within a couple of months, the first copies of Beck's first book, *Pimp: The Story Of My Life* landed on their doorstep in early 1967.

From Pimp To Best Selling Author

Today, many people feel that much of what Beck wrote in *Pimp* is untrue. However, there are several other people who believe that the book's contents in mostly true. One of these people is Mark Skillz, a hip-hop writer, who stated that one of Beck's goals when he started writing the novel, was to be honest. Beck didn't want to glamorize his life or exaggerate in any way. He wanted to write about his life how he lived and saw it. However, because many of the people involved were still alive when Beck wrote his book, he tried to conceal their identities as much as possible, this included his own identity. Therefore, while the situations and personality traits of the friends he made on the streets, such as Satin, were true, Beck did change the names. For instance, Satin became known as Glass Top in Beck's book and Cavanaugh Slim became Iceberg Slim.

For Beck, writing his autobiography was a step in helping him leave that life behind. Now living in California with his family, he didn't want to be Cavanaugh Slim. He wanted to be Robert Beck, or as he was better known to the African American community, Iceberg Slim. For Beck, this autobiography was a way to close the book on that life. As he states in the preface of the book, "Perhaps my remorse for my ghastly life will diminish to the degree that within this one book I have been allowed to purge myself. Perhaps one day I can win respect as a constructive human being."

Once *Pimp: The Story Of My Life* found its way onto the shelves, Beck was surprised at how many books were selling. Even though the book was seen next to Malcolm X's *The Autobiography of Malcolm X*, Beck's writing was different than other African American writers at the time. He wrote about real-life situations in a very cold and raw tone, which is something that most people were not used to. And while Beck's book was met with mixed reviews, the book also started a revolution in the world of pimping.

Beck's dreams about his book becoming a best-seller nearly died because his book received very little publicity for the first year. Holloway House wasn't big in the literary market and many businesses, newspapers, and magazines refused to advertise the book for various reasons. However, once Holloway House decided to advertise in primarily African American magazines, the book's popularity picked up fast and soon Beck found himself thrown into the Hollywood spotlight.

People immediately started requesting Beck to come speak on college campuses. Like Malcolm X's autobiography, Beck's book had become extremely popular in colleges. But, it didn't take long for talk shows, such as *The Black Leader* and *The Louis E Lomax Show* to call Beck to come and do an interview on their show. However, it was *The Joe Pyne Show* that really made people start paying attention to the new author known as Iceberg Slim. However, it wasn't the interview itself that brought Beck into the public eye. It was the publicity stunt that Beck pulled during the interview that got people talking. Betty decided to make him a mask that he would wear while giving the interview. He didn't want to wear it to hide what he looked like, so people wouldn't recognize him on the street. He wore it in order to get people talking about his book. While the couple wasn't sure if it would work, they quickly found that it was one of the best ways to get people talking about not only Beck's autobiography but his first novel, *Trick Baby* at the same time. Within a couple of days, Holloway House' phones were flooded with requests for more books as the stores sold out. The couple finally felt like they had made it.

Some people wondered why Betty and Beck would spend their time pulling a publicity stunt like that? Other people suspected that it was partially because Beck was an African American who was speaking to a primarily white audience. However, many people who have looked into Beck's life disagree with this statement. They believe it had to do with the fact that Beck knew he was skilled at one thing and this was self-promotion. The couple had started to become frustrated with the fact that there was very little publicity for Beck's autobiography. Therefore, they came up with a way that Beck would be able to do his own self-promotion and it worked as Beck's next few books sold well.

After the success of *Pimp: The Story Of My Life*, many other former pimps wrote about their own experiences. On top of this, other people started to write in a bleaker way. Readers started to get an inside look into the world of pimping. Some people became concerned about the life these women were leading. After all, Beck's book was released just a few years before the major 1970's women's rights movement. In fact, Beck's book was still fresh in the minds of many women when the movement started during the 1970s. In fact, some women, such as Hollie West, spoke about taking *Pimp: The Story Of My Life* off the shelves completely and making sure that it could never be sold again.

Other people started to become more interested in the world of pimping, and not because they thought of joining that world. In fact, most didn't envision themselves leading that type of lifestyle. Instead, they wanted to "dig" into the minds of pimps and the women who follow them. In a sense, people wanted to know what made the men and women that followed this type of lifestyle tick. And, of course, one of the first people they would think to discuss the lifestyle with was Robert Beck.

No matter what people thought of Beck's *Pimp: The Story Of My Life*, no one could deny the popularity of the book. By 1973, the book saw over 2 million sales and was on its 19th reprint. Around the same time, the book started to be printed in other languages such as Dutch, Swedish, French, Greek, and German.

Because of the huge success of *Pimp: The Story Of My Life*, people watched for Beck's next book to come out. Fortunately, for his fans, he would continue to write throughout the rest of his life. The same year that *Pimp: The Story Of My Life* was published, Beck's second book, *Trick Baby: The Biography of a Con Man*, a novel, also received publication. However, his second book would not see the fame that his autobiography saw.

Two years later, in 1969, Beck would release his second novel, *Mama Black Widow: A Story of the South's Black Underworld*. This novel discussed the destruction of siblings as they enter the ghetto underworld, where they run into violence, crime, prostitution, and pimping. While this book is one of Beck's fictional works, he takes the world he learned on the streets of Chicago and creates a family to live out its tale.

In 1971, Beck went back to nonfiction, with his second autobiography titled, *The Naked Soul of Iceberg Slim: Robert Beck's Real Story*. This book focuses on who he is in California. Now that people know Iceberg Slim, they are going to learn about the real man behind the notorious former pimp, Robert Beck. Through this book, he showed the world what made him tick. He did this through a collection of essays. The reader gets a sense of what made Beck become a hardened criminal and a violent man towards women. This book gives its readers a sense of how this man known as Iceberg Slim wanted to find a better life for himself and how he continued to have hope that he could change for the better.

In the middle of his writing career, Beck decided to produce an album titled *Reflections*. However, this wasn't your typical album that anyone could have picked up at their local record store. *Reflections* was part of Beck's book, *Pimp: The Story of My Life* which he set to music completed by the Red Holloway Quartet.

In a sense, this album was another way for Beck to reach a different audience. He wanted to do more than get his story out to the public. He wanted to show people not only what his story was like but what life is like on the streets of Chicago.

Like his book, *Pimp,* the album received mixed reviews. Of course, Beck's fans loved the album. They couldn't get enough of him telling his story. In fact, many people stated that Beck was a marvelous storyteller and that he brought the story to life through the spoken word. His emotion was raw and real.

However, other people thought the album was as terrible as the book. No one could deny the tone that Beck used in his writing, which was the same tone he used when bringing his story to life. It was a tone like no other of his time. But it was also a tone that is still used today.

Reflections was Robert Beck's only musical work. He never

even tried to turn his other books into an album. Of course, this only makes Beck's *Pimp: The Story of My Life* more special.

1977 brought another novel from Beck titled, *Long White Con: The Biggest Score of His Life*. This novel was a continuation of Beck's previous novel *Trick Baby: The Biography of a Con Man*. *Long White Con* started where *Trick Baby* left off. Because *Trick Baby* was another one of Beck's hits, it didn't take long for *Long White Con* to make it to the top of the charts for African American authors. For Beck's readers, this novel was another one of his masterpieces which reminded people how brutally honest he could be, whether he was writing a novel or autobiography. Beck became known for telling the truth in a very raw way.

That same year, Holloway House published another novel for Beck, *Death Wish: A Story of the Mafia*. Like Beck's other novels, he took the things he'd learned and saw on the streets to create a powerful and ruthless story about the Chicago mafia. This book has become famous for starting a chain reaction of other Chicago mafia stories.

Robert Beck published *Airtight Willie & Me* in 1985. This book was a collection of stories Beck wrote about those who work and live on the Chicago streets. Many people feel that *Airtight Willie & Me* was Beck's way to not only honor himself and those he knew on Chicago's streets during his time, but also the people who continue to struggle on the streets. Whether they are there because they want to be or because they are forced, Beck wrote a variety of stories detailing the lives people live on the streets. He wrote about con men, prostitutes, and pimps. He wrote about the kind of language they use and the different ways people survive on the streets.

Doom Fox is one of the novels which Beck wrote near the end of his life, but it didn't received publication until a few years after his death. With an introduction by Ice – T, *Doom Fox* follows the basic layout of his other underground novels by bringing out the African American ghetto, crime, and a dysfunctional family. This book follows Joe Allen, who is a heavyweight contender, through his love triangle with a lady named Reba. After driving his father away, Joe marries Reba. Unfortunately, their time together will end in tragedy as Joe catches Reba cheating on him. In response, Joe shoots Reba's lover, which lands him behind bars.

The second novel published posthumously is known as *Shetani's Sister*. This book is a crime novel which takes place on the streets of Los Angeles, California. Shetani, a character in the novel, is a pimp trying to fight back against the LAPD who are trying to clean up the streets. Known as one of the biggest pimps in the novel, Shetani gives readers a look at the life of a pimp who is fighting against police corruption. On the other side, the novel gives readers a look at a member of the

LAPD, Sergeant Russell Rucker, who is determined to decrease the crime of prostitution.

Another novel, *Night Train to Sugar Hill* is set for publication in 2019. This is believed to be Beck's final novel.

While Beck received a lot of praise for his book, he also received a lot of criticism. Of course, some of this criticism came from people who didn't believe such books had to be written, especially when children and teenagers could purchase such a book. But there were other people who didn't care for Robert Beck's writing and one such group was known as the Black Panthers.

The Black Panthers, founded by Huey Newton and Bobby Seale in 1966, was a political party which focused on police brutality against African Americans. They protested the abuse African Americans received from police departments across the United States through armed civilians who joined their political party. When Beck heard about this group in the late 1960s, he praised them for the type of work they were doing. While Beck generally stayed out of the riots and violence that surrounded the Civil Rights Movement, he did lend his support to those who were out there fighting for their rights.

However, once Beck published his first autobiography, he quickly found out that the Black Panthers did not support him. While he didn't let this bother him at first, he eventually did meet up with some members of the party, including Newton. While no one is exactly sure what was said during this meeting, people are aware it had to do with his books and how Beck wrote about young African Americans. Members of the Black Panthers didn't have a problem with his writing style per se, they had a problem with how he portrayed young African Americans. People can assume that whatever happened, it ended in favor of the Black Panthers because after the meeting, Beck wrote less; at least for a period of time.

Through his writing, the former Iceberg Slim became known as one of the masters of African American street literature. He started a new genre in literature which opened up a door for many other writers. While the man who died as Robert Beck didn't always lead the cleanest and best life he could, he worked hard to change his course after finishing his last jail sentence in 1961.

From Novels To Film

There are many best-selling authors whose works have made it onto film and Robert Beck is on this list.

His first book to become a film was the novel *Trick Baby: The Biography of a Con Man* which came to be called *Trick Baby* in 1972. Larry Yust was the director of the film and hired unknown actors to portray the characters, such as Kiel Martin who played the main character "White Folks" and Mel Stewart who played "'Blue' Howard." Produced independently, *Trick Baby* only had a $600,000 budget. Universal Pictures purchased the film for $1,000,000 and set its release date for December of 1972.

Even though no notable actors were a part of the film, Beck's fanbase quickly latched on to the movie. From its time in theaters, *Trick Baby* made over $11 million dollars and received a few good reviews from movie critics. While some critics didn't care too much for the overall acting, they enjoyed the in-depth depiction of race relations within the movie.

For years, another film based on another book of his would be in the works. He would often hide in his bedroom alone in order to work on a screenplay for one of his books. He would then travel to meet different people who said they were interested in helping him produce the film. However, the excitement would die down with very little getting accomplished when it came to Beck's films. Part of the problem was that Hollywood was becoming less interested in the stuff that Beck wrote about. The other part was that Beck really didn't know what he was doing when it came to writing screenplays and making movies. Yes, he was a talented speaker, which made him a talented writer. However, his writing style was very limited and he kept it to the street literature genre, which was a new genre in the entertainment world. Basically, the world was moving on before Beck was ready for it to move on.

Trick Baby is the only book by Robert Beck that's been made into a film. However, his autobiography, *Pimp: The Story of My Life* has been in the works since the 1990s. When news first hit that this book would become Beck's second movie adaptation, Ice Cube was set to star in the film with Bill Duke as director. However, nothing came from the developments. Then, in 2009, Mitch Davis and Rob Weiss purchased the rights to make the film *Pimp*. As of now, nothing has been set in stone for the film.

While his first autobiography has not seen itself on film yet, Jorge Hinojosa directed a documentary in 2012 focusing on Beck. *Iceberg Slim: Portrait of a Pimp* examines the life of Beck, especially his days as a pimp and how he became a best-selling author. The documentary shows interviews from various people, including Beck's daughters, Diane Beck, Betty

(Shue) Beck, Ice - T, and Justin Gifford, who released one of the best biographies on Beck in 2015 titled, *Street Poison: The Biography of Iceberg Slim*.

Chapter 8

End Of An Era

After the success of Beck's first couple of books, he started to change. He was often gone for interviews, book signings, and other speaking engagements. This change in Beck started to frustrate Betty. When he was home, Beck would often lock himself up in a room and focus on writing a new script for a movie he wanted to produce or to work on another book. Betty was supportive of his new career until he started to get into Hollywood, which was a business that neither Beck or Betty understood.

Eventually, the money from the books started to run out and Betty realized she needed to get a job. At the same time, Beck decided that he was going to be done with writing because his last book hadn't seen the success that his first one had. Betty refused to let her husband fall back into his old ways. She told him that if she was going to work, so was he. She was not going to pay his way while he sat on the couch and did nothing. To Betty, this was a step closer to part of his old life and she wanted to keep him away from that. Unfortunately, the couple would not be able to stay together and after months of constant fighting, Betty decided to leave Beck.

Beck was heartbroken about the end of their relationship. He had not only grown to depend on Betty but loved her. However, she had grown to despise Beck. Yes, he was the father of her daughters and had cared for Robin like his own. They had also had several good years together, however, she had grown to hate the man he had become. After she finished packing up her and their children's belongings, Betty told him that if she ever saw his vehicle parked outside of her house, she would throw a match into his gas tank.

Beck was once again starting over in his life. However, this time was very different from any other time. First, Beck was alone and he had never really been alone before. He had either had his mother or someone from his stable to go to when he started over in the past. After his mother died, he had Betty. Second, Beck's health was worsening. A couple of years before Betty left, he found out that he had diabetes. On top of this, he noticed his eyesight was going. He was about 60 years old and hardly able to care for himself. However, he did the best he could because he had no other choice.

The first thing Beck had to do was try to find a job or some way to make money. He was still receiving royalty checks from Holloway House, however, they were quickly decreasing. In fact, by the end of the 1970s, Beck only received a little under $900 from the company for all the books he had published.

But he didn't give up. Beck thought maybe one more book would help him make some more money. After all, he had fans that were not ready to give up on him. Therefore, he released his collection of stories. However, very little money came from that.

Part of the reason Beck started struggling with his writing was because times were changing in Hollywood. People no longer wanted to read or watch movies about the type of lifestyle Beck was portraying. Since Beck's first book, many other people had started writing the same type of books and producing the same type of movies. Hollywood was becoming tired of it; which affected Beck's royalty checks greatly. Around this time, he also found out that the movies people had been planning to produce from his books were no longer in the works. Beck was at a loss for what to do.

Times Are Looking Up

At the beginning of the 1980s, Beck's life started to take a turn for the better. He had received a letter from a fan named Diane Millman. Diane was in her late 30s and had a good job working for the state of California. She considered herself one of his biggest fans and stated that she enjoyed reading his work, especially his last couple of novels. While she wasn't one to write letters to her admirers, she felt the need to write him a letter. In his letter, Diane gave Beck her phone number and told him if he ever wanted to contact her to feel free.

Needless to say, Diane was surprised when she received a call from Beck. It didn't take long for the two to connect. They soon started hanging out and found that they had a lot of common interests. They were both interested in politics, they enjoyed reading the same type of books (of course, Diane loved to read Beck's work), and neither one of them drank. They both enjoyed going to the movies or staying in and watching television at Diane's house. Diane had three children herself, so it was a lot easier for Beck to go to Diane's than anywhere else.

Beck, who was now writing again, depended on Diane to read his work and be honest with her thoughts. At first, he would call her and read a chapter to her every night. Of course, after a while, the couple started to spend more time together and then Beck would either read to her while she was there or she would read it herself. Either way, one of Diane's favorite activities with Beck was to hear his new stories.

After a while, Diane tried to talk Beck into giving his new novel to Holloway House but Beck refused. While he never specifically said why he just told her that he wanted to keep his work away from his publisher. Even if the work was good, and Diane thought it was great, he didn't trust Holloway House like he once had. A part of him felt that they had cheated him out of a lot of money and possibly stopped sending him the royalties that he was owed. After Beck explained his reasoning to her, Diane never pressured him about it again.

The couple continued to grow closer. Within a year after they started dating, Diane helped Beck move in with her. However, he wasn't completely happy with the arrangement. He loved Diane and cared about her children, but he had always enjoyed his time alone. Therefore, Beck purchased a small apartment not far from Diane's house. In 1982, the couple tied the knot – officially. This was the first time Beck had gotten married. He never legally married Betty; she just became his common-law wife. However, he asked Diane to marry him and for the rest of Beck's life, he would remain happily married to Diane.

Unfortunately, Beck continued to be plagued with health

issues. He developed intense pain his legs known as diabetic neuropathy. While Diane did whatever she could to try to help him, the pain started to become too much for Beck. Therefore, Diane brought him to specialists at UCLA Medical Center. Of course, they needed to run tests to find the best course of action to help Beck deal with the pain. During this time, he continued to do what he could to keep himself busy and his mind off the nearly constant pain by writing his next few stories and another novel.

Another thing that kept Beck going through his deteriorating health was the fan mail he continued to receive. Holloway House would forward the mail to him but because Beck was starting to lose his eyesight, Diane would often sit down and read his fan mail to him. He started to notice that the majority of his mail came from people who were or had been in prison and saw him as an inspiration. They felt that if he could turn his life around, then they could do the same thing. He also received fan mail from people who shared similar views or people who sent him some of their work to read. Beck enjoyed the mail and it made him start to feel like he had finally made something good out of his life.

During his later years, Beck struggled with his past and never fully got over all the things he did as a pimp. Not only did he struggle to get over the guilt of what he did to his mother, but he also struggled with the actions and decision he made towards women. The more Beck lived family life, the more he started to regret his past actions. He often talked about how he wished he would have stayed in college and continued to get his degree. Not just because he would have been able to hold down a good job with good pay and wouldn't have had to struggle in his later life, but because he realized that he valued family ways more than he ever thought possible.

However, Beck was now living a life that he felt completely fit him. He loved life with his wife and he continued to enjoy writing the best he could, even if he never planned to publish any of his work again. He not only continued to write novels, but he also wrote short stories. Each one would make its way to Diane, who would give Beck her impression of the writing.

In the mid-1980s, Beck started to spend more time alone in his own little apartment. It's not that he felt his marriage was in trouble, he simply enjoyed being alone and this became more of a theme in his later years. His health was continuing to deteriorate and, at times, this would start to depress him. On top of that, Beck had always enjoyed his time alone. Even when he was living in Chicago as a pimp, he had a house for his girls (sometimes he did well enough that he had a few different places for his women) and then he had his own place, which was generally a hotel. During the time he lived with Betty, he had his own room where he could be alone with his work and thoughts.

While Diane missed Beck when he was gone, she also knew that he wasn't that far away and understood his desire to have his own place. She remained happy in their marriage and would continue to do whatever she could in order to make the rest of his life comfortable whether he was at her house or at his own apartment. She even went to Beck's apartment to help him organize it. He didn't have much but he also didn't need much. The man who had once dreamed of living the luxurious lifestyle was now satisfied in a tiny studio apartment with a large bed so he could comfortably write and have work spread out, a recliner near a window that allowed him to watch people on the street, a couple of other chairs, a dresser, and pictures of his family.

Beck started to become very well-known around the neighborhood. He could often be seen in his window with his binoculars as he watched the children play in the street or people walk to and from one place to the next. Beck had turned into a writer and often used this time to be with his thoughts, which would lead him to produce more short stories.

While the younger generation enjoyed having Beck around, it was the older generation that really enjoyed Beck's company. He would often get older people visiting because they remembered his books and wanted to stop to pay their respects to someone who used to be or was one of their favorite authors. Many people in the African American community had started seeing Beck as more of a legacy than a person. He had paved the way for a new type of literature. He had been one of the many authors to write about race relations and discuss the truth that many people were too afraid, especially during the 1960s, to discuss. Some people who respected him would stop by just to bring him some weed. While Beck stopped drinking during the early 1960s, he did smoke weed every now and then. He saw no problem in smoking a bit of weed with a fan or with his wife.

When he could, people would find Beck out walking. He would often take a long walk, where he would find himself talking with people in the neighborhood. Sometimes, he would get into long discussions about politics, race relations, or other worldly issues. Unfortunately, as the years went by, people would see less and less of Beck outside. His health continued to cause him problems, especially the pain in his legs. On top of that, his organs were slowly shutting down. In the late 1980s, the doctors told Beck that his kidneys were failing. At this point, both Beck and Diane knew that it was only a matter of time.

However, Beck didn't let that stop him. He continued to dress his best and write as much as he could. Unfortunately, in the last few years of his life, Beck's eyesight started to deteriorate even more. This made him more depressed because he could no longer take a major role in the last couple of things he found great pleasure in, writing and watching the people on the street. After his death, Diane would say that while he never went fully blind, his eyesight was bad enough that he couldn't really read. Therefore, she would visit him and read some of her favorite books to him. On top of this, she would often write down some of his ideas for stories.

Beck: Everyone's Father Figure

In the last few years of his life, he was able to have a relationship with some of his children. While his son didn't want anything to do with him, his daughters would visit. Beck knew that his past had an effect on his children, and this didn't surprise him. They didn't have to read his autobiography in order to know that, at one point, he was one of the most notorious pimps on the streets of Chicago. They would hear about their father through his fans or other people, simply because they were the children of Iceberg Slim.

Beck had always done his best to be a part of his children's lives. He even went to support Misty when she had to go to court because she got caught drinking at the age of fifteen. However, he had the most trouble with his oldest daughter. Unfortunately, she inherited most of her father's bad habits and started hitting the streets at an early age. In the mid-

1980s, he helped Camille when she got in legal trouble. Beck did his best to be there for his children, whether they just wanted to visit or had gotten into some sort of legal trouble. However, this could never overcome the complicated relationship he would continue to have with them for the rest of his life.

Even though some of his own children struggled with his past, Beck continued to be an inspiration and sometimes a father figure to many other people. Some of these people had read his books while others had met him through one of his walks and hearing people talk about an "Iceberg Slim" and they had come to form a connection with him. Whenever someone who was in need of a friend came knocking on Beck's door, he was happy to invite them in and be that friend. In a sense, this was another way that Beck was able to turn his life around and help him feel less guilty about the past and the life he once led. Of course, he would always hold some type of guilt about his past, especially for the way he treated his mother, however, he tried to help ease his mind by helping others in his later life.

Beck would become a father figure or inspiration to not just people he met on his walks but also many people who would become famous. One of these people is Mike Tyson, who had read Beck's books and considered him one of his biggest influences. Tyson would often visit Beck at his apartment where they would talk about various things, especially the trouble Tyson had with women. Beck understood Tyson and tried to give him advice to help him. Unfortunately, the advice would not go very far as Tyson would find himself in legal trouble for assaulting women.

After Beck's death, Tyson often spoke about their time together. He discussed how he felt that Beck was a true pimp to his dying day. While Tyson was always willing to help Beck with whatever he needed, especially financially, Beck never really took anything from Tyson. He was content in his small apartment with his few belongings. However, he did ask Tyson to help him when it came to planning his funeral. Tyson later recalled that when he did help Beck, he never received any sort of thank you. Instead, Beck just told him that he thought it was cool that he was willing to help him. To Tyson, this is what made him enjoy Beck's company and look up to him as an inspiration. No matter what was going on or how old Beck was, he kept it all real. He didn't hide anything he did in his life and he didn't flaunt anything. He was realistic to the very end.

Beck's Growing Concerns For The African American Community

One thing that never changed throughout Beck's life was his concern for the African American community. In fact, the older he got, the more concern he felt. He knew first-hand what it was like to live in a segregated world and even though the days of legal segregation were gone, Beck found that the Los Angeles Police Department were once again getting rough with the African American communities. While there had always been some racism within the black and white communities, Beck felt that the tension was growing and he feared that this would bring America, or at least Los Angeles, into another phase of riots.

Beck was well aware that the riots of 1965 caused the police in the area to become more heavily armed and more cautious of the African American communities. He knew that after the riots, the police started to increase their presence around Beck's community and that they started putting more money into surveillance equipment. Beck also realized that it was this ever-growing police presence that caused many younger African Americans to despise police officers. They started to feel more like targets because of something that had happened years ago. On top of this, while segregation had become illegal, it was still heavily present. Beck knew this as well as most other African Americans in the community and, once again, a majority of them were starting to fight back.

Now, instead of fighting the laws of America, African Americans were beginning to fight the police officers in America. On top of this, the 1980s saw a spike in unemployment, which caused more problems on the streets of Beck's community. The jobs that were available we very low-paying and continued to keep families in poverty. Many people started to resort to stealing or breaking the law in other ways in order to get by. This brought an increase in gang-related activity, prostitution, and other crimes. Hearing about this increase at the end of his life bothered Beck. He felt that parts of life were moving in the wrong direction, almost like they were going back in time, and this worried him. Not only did he worry for what this would do to the community as a whole, but he worried about the children that were out on the streets.

While Beck felt that he couldn't help the African American communities in their disputes with the LAPD, he knew that he could have some impact on the young kids who were walking around the streets in his own community. While he rarely went outside anymore, many of the kids would come and see him. Some of them came to discuss their problems while others came to see if they could help Beck in any way. Through their conversations, Beck learned that gangs were becoming a problem. He heard about how many gangs were trying to recruit young members because they felt they would need more members to keep tabs on the police.

Beck became worried about the direction some of the kids on the street were going. He didn't want them to follow in his path. This was always a bit of a worry when people came to him saying they idolized him because he had been such a big hustler in his time. On top of following the pimp lifestyle, he also didn't want anyone joining a gang or getting in with the wrong crowd. While Beck spent a lot of time in his younger days causing problems on the streets, he wanted to spend his later years doing what he could to clean up the streets, especially in the African American communities.

Therefore, Beck came up with an idea that started with the kids who came to visit him. He would start to keep the kids busy by giving them certain tasks to do. While he didn't have a lot of money to pay them well, he did have a few quarters he could always spare and he knew that the kids who helped him would love to receive a quarter or two as payment. However, there was one kid he spent a little more time on than other. This kid came to be known as "Key" and had already found himself on the wrong side of the streets.Key came to Beck in hopes that he could help him turn his life around. Key didn't want to spend his life in and out of jail and struggling to get by. Unfortunately, Beck would not be able to help Key like both of them hoped, as the law finally caught up to Key and he received a life sentence for robbery.

However, Beck's time was coming to an end. His health was getting worse as he had now been diagnosed with an enlarged heart and was completely blind in one eye. He no longer allowed as many people to visit and would rarely step foot outside. However, through it all, Beck did his best to remain positive and not complain about his health. While he continued to worry about his financial stability, Diane assured him that everything would be taken care of. Without Beck knowing, Diane went to Holloway House and asked them to give an advance on Beck's next royalty check. She knew that he wouldn't last much longer and she wanted to do everything she could to make his last days comfortable and give him less to worry about.

During Beck's final days, the Rodney King riots started. They were the riots that Beck knew were coming. A part of him feared these riots, yet there was also a part of him which was pleased by their arrival. He wanted better for African Americans and he knew that one of the ways they could do this was through riots. In his final days, Beck laid in a hospital bed watching the riots unfold on the television.

The day was April 30, 1992, and the riots had created havoc in the city of Los Angeles. Inside the hospital, Diane and Beck found out that he had an infection in his leg and in order for him to live, they would have to remove his foot and part of his leg. Beck was old and had been in ill health for some time, so he was unsure that he wanted to go through such an operation. He asked them to run some tests, so they did. However, the tests wouldn't be ready until the following day.

That evening, Beck went into cardiac arrest. While the doctors tried to save them, there was nothing they could do. Robert Beck was laid to rest on May 9th, with over 100 people in attendance.

While Beck's life was now over, the struggles for his wife and children would continue. A few years ago, Diane and his daughters filed a lawsuit against Holloway House for unpaid royalties. Diane stated that Beck died penuriously and should have been given a lot more in royalties than he was sent, per the contract.

A few years after his death, Diane took a manuscript to a different publishing company. While Beck never wanted to publish again in his life, she felt that his talent needed to be seen by the world once more. While she had to offer the manuscript to Holloway House before any other publishing company due to Beck's contract, she never had to agree to let them publish the work, and she didn't. Instead, she allowed Grove Press to publish it. Of course, she had to deal with a variety of legal troubles before publication, such as Holloway House questioning her rights to the book and questioning whether Beck had written the book himself or not.

However, none of the trouble that Diane went through would dampen her dreams to see her husband's work get into the hands of his fans. After all, Diane knew how much Beck's fans meant to him and how much he meant to his fans. It was

Diane that often read Beck his fan mail in his later years when he could barely see. On top of that, the couple would often spend time reading the fan mail together. While some people criticized Diane for exploiting her husband after death or just wanting to cash in, this was never her intention. She always felt that Beck had a natural gift for writing and she wanted him to continue to share it with the world. But, she also knew he refused because of the treatment he received from his publisher.

Diane would go on to publish more works by her husband over the years. However, to this day, no one is sure just how many novels and short stories Beck never published. No one is sure if all his work will ever be published or not. However, what people are sure of is no matter what novel or short story is published or when, his fans will continue to read his work. On top of that, a younger generation will start to pick up the works of Robert Beck and begin to learn about the underground world during Beck's time and find someone who worked hard to become the best person he could be at the end of his life.

Chapter 9

The Legacy Iceberg Slim Left Behind

During his days as Iceberg Slim, no one imagined the legacy that he would leave behind. After all, how could someone who was ruthless and violent leave a lasting legacy for the world? He would do anything to make it to the top as a pimp and when he made it there, he would do anything to stay there. He never gave a thought about what he was doing to other people, he fell into the world of drugs and sex and he had intended to stay there for the rest of his life. However, after spending decades between the streets of Milwaukee, Chicago, and jail, Iceberg Slim turned his life around when he became known as Robert Beck.

Beck's is not your typical rags to riches story. In fact, you could argue his story isn't a rag to riches story as he died penniless. Even though he became a best-selling author and his books are still being re-printed today, Beck had little to show from his chart-topping days, he never saw the extreme wealth many other authors see. However, this doesn't mean that Beck has little to show when it comes to his legacy. Beck's legacy goes beyond any of the wealth he saw in his life. It goes beyond any of the struggles he faced or the fact that he became one of the top pimps on the streets of Chicago in the 1950s. Beck's legacy focuses on the doors he opened for other people. It focuses on how he decided he would expose the underworld of pimping. It focuses on how someone who was going down the road to becoming another pimp that led a short life and no one would remember, became someone whose books have been on the shelves for decades. Beck's legacy focuses on someone who, without a college education or a stable job was able to change the lives of other people. And, at the end of his life, all he had to do was sit in his apartment and wait for people to come to him. Beck's legacy focuses on a man who tried to change the world the best way he could, by telling his story and then finding ways to help the kids who came to him.

Beck spent years turning his life around. He spent years focusing on finding a way to provide for his family and become the best husband and father he could. While his life as Robert Beck did have its share of problems, it also showed people that they didn't have to stay on the streets of Chicago. It showed people that they could lead a better life, they just had to want to.

Another reason why Beck's stories because so popular was because people were able to relate to his autobiography.

When people are looking for someone to inspire them or looking for someone to become their role model, they are looking for someone who they can relate to. Through his books, people were able to relate to what Beck wrote about. They could relate to the dysfunctional family, getting addicted to cocaine, growing up without a father, or trying to find their place in the world. People could relate to the internal struggle Beck wrote about in his autobiography. The struggle of being frustrated with his mother yet having a deep love for her at the same time.

This is one reason Ice - T felt inspired by Beck, as he stated, "[Iceberg] didn't start writing books until he was out of the game... Well, I didn't start making music until I was out of the game. To watch him transform into this person that tries to help kids and warn them against life on the street, that's the same thing I do." When people can relate to someone, it gives them the confidence and determination they need in order to continue on their journey. It helps them so they don't feel alone. Furthermore, when they look up to that person, it helps them feel that they are doing something right because, in their mind, the person they look up to did something right.

But, Beck's legacy goes beyond letting those living on the streets know they can make a living off the streets. His legacy brought out the truth of street life. And this is one of the things Beck wanted his first autobiography to do. He wanted to show people how dehumanizing the lifestyle of pimping was. Beck wasn't proud of his days on the streets of Chicago and he didn't want to see anyone fall into that life. While many people felt Beck's book, *Pimp* glamourized the lifestyle, this was far from Beck's goal. He didn't want people to fall for the lifestyle, he wanted people to walk away from that lifestyle. Furthermore, through telling his story, Beck hoped that people would see they could walk away from that lifestyle - for good.

Robert Beck's legacy does not end there. Through his writing, Beck brought out a new genre in English literature known as "street literature" or Urban Fiction. Through his work, Beck opened the door for many other authors of street literature. Without Robert Beck, *Addicted* by Zane, *The Coldest Winter Ever* by Sister Souljah, *A Hustler's Wife* by Nikki Turner, or *The Family Business* by Carl Weber may not have been published. Today, Urban Fiction is one of the most popular literary genres and we all have Robert Beck to thank for it. He was one of the pioneer authors of the genre thanks to his autobiographies, novels, and short stories. In fact, many authors who write Urban Fiction, often point to one of Robert Beck's books as a source of inspiration.

Finally, another part of Beck's legacy is the husband and father he became. While he had a bit of a strained relationship with at least some of his kids, he always tried to do his best.

He might not have been able to hold his children and often want a kiss as most parents do. He might not have been able to play outside with his kids without worrying about something happening to them and losing his temper as most parents do, but he always did what he could for them. In his autobiography, Pimp, he discusses that his family is one of the main reasons for the book. While he only had his oldest two children when he wrote the book, he talks highly of them at the end. He discusses how he works as hard as he does for them. He also discusses that he does what he does in this "square world" in order for them to have a better life than he did. He then goes on to discuss how the mother of his children, Betty, is one of the most amazing mothers and he couldn't have asked for a better mother for his children.

When you read the end of Beck's first autobiography, you can't deny his change. When you think back to how he treated women during his days as a pimp and then read the last part of the book where he is talking about his family, you can't deny the effort and strength Beck had in order to do whatever he could to make sure he turned his life around, not only for himself but for Betty, his children, and his mother. It isn't easy to make these types of changes, especially when you are so used to a certain lifestyle. Beck could have easily found his way back onto the streets and into the underground pimping world after his mother died or he started his family. But he decided to do whatever he could, including living nearly penniless, in order to remain the changed man.

Right after his death, it seemed that the books Robert Beck wrote would soon be gone and lost in history. However, there were many people who refused to let this happen. Because of gangsta rappers, Robert Beck's memory continues today. Rapper Ice - T has paid homage to Robert Beck many times. For example, his 1989 album, The Iceberg/Freedom of Speech... Just Watch What You Say! is dedicated to Beck's legacy and image. This album is full of some of Ice-T's darkest music and caused censorship issues after its release. On top of this, Ice-T's name is a tribute to Iceberg Slim. Other people who have paid tribute with Iceberg Slim's name are Ice Cube, Pittsburgh Slimm, and Iceberg Slimm. In fact, Robert Beck's legacy has only grown over the last few years and not just because of gangsta rappers like Ice – T or Ice Cube. Over the last few years, his books have been published again and are now available online.

Lately, the online world has started to take a look at Iceberg Slim. Over the past few years, writers have started to focus their attention on Beck's biography. In 2015, *Street Poison: The Biography of Iceberg Slim* by Justin Gifford became one of the first official biographies on Iceberg Slim. Gifford not only used Beck's own autobiographies for his book, but he also contacted people who had known Beck to gain a better understanding of him. Through his research, Gifford has created the most in-depth biography on Beck to date.

Another biography, written by Dennis Smith called *Iceberg Slim: The Biography of a Pimp* came out in 2018 and is another well-written and in-depth biography on Robert Beck. These two biographies are only the tip of the iceberg when it comes to people who are focusing on the man who became known as Iceberg Slim.

Conclusion

Nearly everything you've learned about the life of pimps came from Robert Beck's autobiography, *Pimp: The Story Of My Life*. Before this book, people knew very little about the world of pimping. While many people believe Beck made pimping famous, he really only brought the world of pimping out from the underground. Men had been pimps long before Beck joined the streets, it's just they were able to follow their chosen career path without everyone looking their way. Now, people are always questioning what is happening to women who stand on the street corner. People are wondering about the men who look like Slim did as he was on the streets of Milwaukee and Chicago. The police pay more attention and the world of pimping is a common theme in crime shows like *Law and Order: SVU*.

Robert Beck is a person who painted his portrait the colors he wanted to. He was an intelligent man who spent a good part of his life as a pimp on the streets of Chicago because of a growing adoration of the lifestyle. He then changed his life's path in his later years to focus on writing. For the first part of his life, no one could imagine that Beck would pass away with the legacy he holds today.

For some people, it's hard to understand how someone who became known as such a hardened pimp and criminal could become so influential to many people. However, if you take a deeper look at Beck's life, you can start to see why. As an author, he paved the way for many people. On top of this, he showed the African American community that you can become anything you set your mind to, no matter what your past holds.

When Robert Beck published his first book, *Pimp: The Story of my Life* in 1967, he paved a new road for African Americans during a time when the country was divided. They were fighting for their equality rights when Beck soared onto the writing scene. Of course, many places wouldn't sell or advertise Beck's book for many reasons. First, he was a former pimp. Second, his writing opened the world up to Chicago's streets and crime. Third, he was African American. However, this didn't stop Beck from selling millions of books within a few years. While the white communities mostly ignored Beck's book at first, the African American communities dived right in. They couldn't get enough of the former pimp known as Iceberg Slim.

Eventually, other people would find Beck's works an interesting read. They were a different version of literature.

One which had never been written before but had started a wave of other authors who focused on "street literature."

While Robert Beck might not be remembered as many other authors of his time, such as Kurt Vonnegut, Agatha Christie, or John Updike, this doesn't make his work any less important. In fact, Beck became one of the most successful African American authors of his day. While he might not have sold the most books among African American authors, he did something that most authors never do – he established a new genre in literature. He opened the door for other people who wanted to write about the underground world. Furthermore, he did this during a time when most African Americans were struggling for their civil rights. Beck was able to break some of society's molds without meaning to. He never knew that once he published his first book, that he would create something for generations to come. In fact, at first, he wasn't even sure that anyone would want to read it.

On top of this, his work remains influential for many people in the Hip Hop and African American communities. To this day, people are reading his books not only to learn about the world that once was but to gain a sense of accomplishment from someone who worked in a career where people generally died of drug overdoses or end up in prison for the rest of their lives, which most of Beck's friends from his days as Slim did. His life remains influential to people because it gives them a sense of hope when they feel lost in the world. It lets them know that no matter where they are at this moment in their life, whether it's in prison or homeless on the street, they can make something of their lives. They can turn their lives around and help other people. They don't have to stay on the streets. Once they get released from prison, they don't need to become one of the statistics that end back up in the prison system. When people feel they are at the lowest point in their lives is when people need inspiration the most in order to keep going. Robert Beck is the person that gives many people this inspiration. And this is one reason, after his years of struggling, jail life, life on the streets, and illness he died a fulfilled and happy man. Because he was able to give so many people something in this world that he felt was missing from his life when he was at his lowest – hope and inspiration that he could change.

With more of Robert Beck's books getting published, people will continue to read the life and works of Beck. And with the increase of interest on the internet, it doesn't look like Beck's legacy will disappear any time soon.

Printed in Great Britain
by Amazon